How to access the supplemental web re

We are pleased to provide access to a web resource that suppleme... ....,
Beginning Modern Dance. This resource offers photos and video clips of modern dance
techniques, learning activities, assignments, quizzes, and much more.

Accessing the web resource is easy!
Follow these steps if you purchased a new book:

1. Visit **www.HumanKinetics.com/BeginningModernDance**.

2. Click the <u>first edition</u> link next to the book cover.

3. Click the Sign In link on the left or top of the page. If you do not have an
   account with Human Kinetics, you will be prompted to create one.

4. If the online product you purchased does not appear in the Ancillary Items box
   on the left of the page, click the Enter Key Code option in that box. Enter the
   key code that is printed at the right, including all hyphens. Click
   the Submit button to unlock your online product.

5. After you have entered your key code the first time, you will never have to
   enter it again to access this product. Once unlocked, a link to your product will
   permanently appear in the menu on the left. For future visits, all you need to
   do is sign in to the textbook's website and follow the link that appears in the
   left menu!

→ Click the Need Help? button on the textbook's website if you need assistance along
   the way.

How to access the web resource if you purchased a used book:

You may purchase access to the web resource by visiting the text's website,
www.HumanKinetics.com/BeginningModernDance, or by calling the following:

800-747-4457 . . . . U.S. customers
800-465-7301 . . . . Canadian customers
+44 (0) 113 255 5665 . . . . European customers
08 8372 0999 . . . . Australian customers
0800 222 062 . . . . New Zealand customers
217-351-5076 . . . . International customers

For technical support, send an e-mail to:
support@hkusa.com . . . . U.S. and international customers
info@hkcanada.com . . . . Canadian customers
academic@hkeurope.com . . . . European customers
keycodesupport@hkaustralia.com . . . . .Australian and New Zealand customers

HUMAN KINETICS
Th(

Health

12-2013

467 663 67 5

This unique code allows you access to the web resource.

Access is provided if you have purchased a new book.
Once submitted, the code may not be entered for any
other user.

Product: Beginning Modern Dance web resource
Key code: GIGUERE-9YG4PP-OSG

D0320809

Beginning
MODERN DANCE

INTERACTIVE DANCE SERIES

Miriam Giguere, PhD

Drexel University, Philadelphia

Human Kinetics

Library of Congress Cataloging-in-Publication Data

Giguere, Miriam
  Beginning modern dance / Miriam Giguere.
    pages cm. -- (Interactive dance series)
  Includes bibliographical references and index.
  1. Modern dance I. Title.
  GV1783.G48 2014
  792.8--dc23

2013010166

ISBN-10: 1-4504-0517-7 (print)
ISBN-13: 978-1-4504-0517-1 (print)

Portions of chapters 1 through 3 are adapted from Gayle Kassing, 2013, *Beginning ballet* (Champaign, IL: Human Kinetics); Lisa Lewis, 2013, *Beginning tap dance* (Champaign, IL: Human Kinetics).

The web addresses cited in this text were current as of June 11, 2013, unless otherwise noted.

Acquisitions Editor: Gayle Kassing, PhD; **Developmental Editor:** Bethany Bentley; **Assistant Editor:** Derek Campbell; **Copyeditor:** Jan Feeney; **Indexer:** Sharon Duffy; **Permissions Manager:** Dalene Reeder; **Graphic Designer:** Joe Buck; **Graphic Artist:** Yvonne Griffith; **Cover Designer:** Keith Blomberg; **Photographer (cover and interior):** Bernard Wolff, unless otherwise noted; p. 101 © Keystone-France/Gamma-Keystone via Getty Images; pp. 105, 106, 108, 115 Jerome Robbins Dance Division, New York Public Library for the Performing Arts, Astor, Lenox and Tilden Foundations; pp. 116, 121 ©Julie Lemberger/CORBIS; **Visual Production Assistant:** Joyce Brumfield; **Photo Production Manager:** Jason Allen; **Art Manager:** Kelly Hendren; **Associate Art Manager:** Alan L. Wilborn; **Illustrations:** © Human Kinetics; **Printer:** Versa Press

We thank Drexel University in Philadelphia, Pennsylvania, for providing the location for the photo shoot for this book.

Printed in the United States of America   10 9 8 7 6 5 4 3 2 1

The paper in this book is certified under a sustainable forestry program.

Human Kinetics
Website: www.HumanKinetics.com

United States: Human Kinetics
P.O. Box 5076
Champaign, IL 61825-5076
800-747-4457
e-mail: humank@hkusa.com

Canada: Human Kinetics
475 Devonshire Road Unit 100
Windsor, ON N8Y 2L5
800-465-7301 (in Canada only)
e-mail: info@hkcanada.com

Europe: Human Kinetics
107 Bradford Road
Stanningley, Leeds LS28 6AT, United Kingdom
+44 (0) 113 255 5665
e-mail: hk@hkeurope.com

Australia: Human Kinetics
57A Price Avenue
Lower Mitcham, South Australia 5062
08 8372 0999
e-mail: info@hkaustralia.com

New Zealand: Human Kinetics
P.O. Box 80, Torrens Park, South Australia 5062
0800 222 062
e-mail: info@hknewzealand.com

E5332

This book is dedicated to Ralph, Natalie, William, and Andrew Giguere, each an artist and scholar in his or her own right, whose support has been the foundation of any successful projects in which I have engaged.

Contents

8 Five Major Styles of Modern Dance 125

Preface

Modern dance as a performing art was created out of a need for change. It developed at the beginning of the 20th century when women were looking to find a new way to express themselves as independent members of society, modern artists were looking for innovative ways to explore human experience through abstraction, and changes in society were happening at an increasingly rapid pace. Modern dance was born in a time of change and has continued to embrace the idea that art can reflect this change in society and in the individual. The study of modern dance is not merely learning new ways to move. It is also about embarking on a personal journey to explore and reflect the changes in yourself and in the world around you.

This book will give you the information you need for success in modern dance class. Chapter 1 looks at the specifics of how a modern dance class is run and the principles of the genre. Chapter 2 explains how to prepare for class physically and mentally. Chapter 3 provides a guide to safety, nutrition, and injury prevention. Chapter 4 reviews the concepts and movement principles in modern dance. Chapter 5 covers the basics of creating dance, also known as dance composition. Chapter 6 addresses how to view and respond to dance performances. Chapter 7 offers an overview of the 100-year history of modern dance. Finally, chapter 8 connects this history to technique class by outlining five major styles of modern dance. This textbook will help you to see the philosophy of the body that underlies the modern dance class you are taking and find your own artistic voice in the process.

Sections of the text are also devoted to the practical needs of dancers, such as how to prevent injury, how to warm up for class, and how to keep your body in shape for dancing. This book also provides guidelines for mindful practices in technique class. The basics of creating choreographic studies and viewing modern dance are also covered so that you have a fuller picture of the genre.

The web resource that accompanies this book offers supplemental interactive instruction. Visit **www.HumanKinetics.com/BeginningModernDance1E** to check it out. The web resource provides you with added opportunities to practice the steps and techniques explained in this book.

The aim of modern dance is to give dancers a vocabulary for developing their creative and expressive potential. This book will help you find your own voice through modern dance by understanding the history, philosophy, and fundamentals of this performing art form.

Acknowledgments

Special thanks to Jenna Boyes, Susan Deutsch, Olive Prince, and Saroya Corbett, who all reviewed sections of the text and lent their support and expertise. Thanks also to Rachel Ragland, whose support and example gave me the courage to undertake this book, and to the dance students at Drexel University over the past 20 years who have given their hearts, minds, and bodies to the pursuit of artistic and personal development through modern dance.

How to Use the Web Resource

In a modern dance class, exercises and combinations can move quickly. They can also contain a large number of new movements or small additions to existing movements you have learned. However, you have an added advantage! Your personal tutor is just a few clicks away and is always available to help you remember and practice the exercises and steps executed in class. You can study between class meetings or when you are doing mental practice to memorize exercises or movement. Check out the book's accompanying web resource at **www.HumanKinetics.com/ BeginningModernDance1E.**

The web resource is an interactive tool that can be used to enhance understanding of beginning modern dance technique, review of what was studied in class, or prepare for performance testing. It includes information about each exercise or movement, including notes for correct performance; photos of foot and arm positions; and video clips of modern dance techniques. Also included are interactive quizzes for each chapter of your *Beginning Modern Dance* text, which let you test your knowledge of concepts, modern dance basics, terminology, and more.

In a beginning modern dance class, students learn about modern technique, modern dance as an art form, and themselves. The Supplementary Materials section of the web resource contains the following additional components for each chapter of your *Beginning Modern Dance* text. These components support both learning in the modern dance class and exploring more about the world of modern dance.

- Glossary terms from the text are presented so that you can check your knowledge of the translated meaning of the term as well as a description of the term.
- Web links give you a starting place to learn more about modern dance techniques, styles, or dance companies.
- Chapters include e-journaling prompts, handouts and assignments to think more deeply about beginning modern dance class.
- Other assignments include specific activities to apply the concepts and ideas about modern dance.

We hope that the web resource helps you to individualize your learning experience so that you can connect to, expand, and apply your learning of beginning tap dance, enhancing your success and enjoyment in your study of this dance form.

1

Introduction to Modern Dance

Welcome to the art of modern dance! The class you are taking will be a journey into an art form that will teach you not only new movements but also new ideas. You will learn to respond to music with your body, gain greater control over your movements, build strength, and navigate space with other dancers. Modern dance, as you will learn, is not just a physical practice but also a form of expression. For more than a century, dancers have entered spaces like the one in which you have class to learn to refine their ability to express ideas and emotions through the vocabulary of modern dance. This chapter begins with an overview of modern dance and what you can expect to do in a beginning modern dance technique class.

DEFINING MODERN DANCE

Modern dance is a term that describes many types of dance techniques. Rather than being one style, modern dance is a category of dance styles, often referred to as a **genre** of dance. Many of the main styles in this genre are credited to specific choreographers who pioneered ways of moving and new **movement vocabularies** based on their personal philosophies (their views of how dance functions as an artistic tool). Graham, Humphrey-Limón, Dunham, Horton, and Cunningham techniques are examples of modern dance styles that were created by prominent 20th-century choreographers. The term *modern* was used to describe these dance forms, in part, because they have their roots in the modernist movement of the early 20th century. This was a spirit of change in art, music, design, and theater that represented a shift from the existing traditions in art forms toward new ideas that mirrored the modernization and industrialization of society. It promoted the idea that abstract representation, in addition to narrative (storytelling), was to be valued. It was also connected to a spirit of change that stretched beyond art and included the beginnings of the women's movement and other political and social changes. The idea of reflecting change in the culture is still an important part of modern dance. The art form evolved through a series of transformations led by dynamic individuals who rebelled against aspects of society and the current structures of concert dance. These rebels of the art form, as you will learn, were driven to find new ways to express themselves. This spirit of rebellion and change is still a part of modern dance today.

When hearing the term *modern dance*, many dancers think it means a new art form. On the contrary, modern dance is over 100 years old. It is certainly newer than ballet, which dates to the 17th century and King Louis XIV, but it is not necessarily a new form. While rooted in the early part of the 20th century, modern dance is still a vibrant and expanding art form. Many new and hybrid forms of modern dance are being created every day. Some are fusions of styles created by the masters of the genre from the 1930s and '40s. Others are fusions of modern dance and other genres, such as jazz, ballet, hip-hop, African, and postmodern dance.

Dancers trained in private dance studios often tend to associate modern dance with the terms **lyrical** or **contemporary** dance. While these studio and competition forms might have some movements in common with professional concert modern dance, lyrical dance actually refers to a quality of movement. A lyrical movement is fluid (that is, continuous) and often musically performed. The dances you learned in your studio lyrical class may be closer to contemporary ballet, or they could be the kind of modern dance that showcases this quality in the choreography. Similarly, contemporary usually means that it has been created recently; is performed to contemporary music; is a fusion of ballet, jazz, and modern styles; or is intended to be a reflection of contemporary life through dance. Some modern dance fits this definition, but other kinds, based on the traditional, original modern dance styles, do not.

What, then, makes something *modern* dance? No absolute lines are drawn in the world of professional dance, and by studying multiple styles of dance, many dancers train their bodies to be versatile tools for choreographers. But for the purposes of this textbook, and to make your transition into modern dance class a success, we limit our definition of modern dance to forms that have at least one of the following characteristics:

◆ Based on one of the codified techniques of the early masters, such as Graham, Humphrey-Limón, Dunham, Horton, or Cunningham

◆ Based on movements created by use of the breath, articulation of the torso (such as aligned, tilted, or contracted), use of the floor, or improvisation, without the need for turned-out positions of the legs or pointed feet

◆ A fusion of dance styles that use the movement vocabulary of ballet, jazz, modern, hip-hop, Afro-Caribbean, capoeira, and postmodern dance in the same choreography

◆ A strong association with the ground in movement choices; an emphasis on grounded movement when standing and a vocabulary of movements done while lying or seated on the floor

Modern dance is a changing and vibrant form of physical expression. As you become more familiar with the art form, you will learn about the variety of dance movements that make up modern dance and sense the breadth of ideas that are included in this genre. Perhaps you will even detect the spirit of change that gave birth to this kind of dance.

BENEFITS OF STUDYING MODERN DANCE

Dance is often described as the synthesis of body, mind, and spirit. All three of these aspects are reasons to study modern dance. Like any dance discipline, modern dance can develop muscle control, strength, flexibility, aerobic capacity, and an overall sense of physical well-being. Modern dance students gain an awareness of how their bodies work to express and communicate ideas and feelings and can develop a sensitivity toward the body language of others.

An increased mental awareness is also a frequent positive result of studying dance. Regular dance classes can improve your ability to concentrate, particularly if you work in a careful and reflective way as described in this book. The practice of focusing on a regular basis during technique class may increase your mental stamina for concentration. Learning to pick up unfamiliar movement sequences quickly—which will eventually be required of you in modern dance classes—can increase your capacity for observation. The use of improvisation, so common in modern classes, improves your ability to think on your feet, sharpening both mind and body.

Modern dancers often find that the spiritual benefits of this art form are just as powerful as the development of body and mind. The ability to safely release your emotions and feel psychological well-being as a result is called catharsis. Many dancers experience this feeling by fully engaging the mind and body through dance. Students who feel the pressures of their education find release in coming to the studio and dancing it out. In addition to the immediate joy that is felt after dancing, an ongoing personal development can take place. Dancers who attend to the connection between the body's ability to communicate and their inner concerns begin to develop an **artistic voice**. This is each person's unique ability to explore issues and ideas in the world through abstract conceptualizations. Expression through the medium of modern dance is one path to development of artistic voice. Each dancer comes to learn how he or she likes to move—fast, slow, traveling, in the air, on the floor—and how that changes from day to day according to moods or experiences. Dancers begin to understand what movements hold the most personal meaning for them and which types of dance seem the most natural. Discovering your movement preferences through the variety of movements that are used in a modern dance class is another step toward your growth as an artist and as a person. You might discover that one style of modern dance resonates more deeply with you than another, and just as often it is because the worldview, or philosophy, that underlies the technique is in alignment with your beliefs. Learning the aesthetic ideas that lie beneath the traditional forms of modern dance can help you clarify your own philosophy on life.

BASICS OF MODERN DANCE CLASS

The three partners that make the modern dance technique class a success are the teacher, the musician, and the students. All three have specific roles to fulfill in making a fun, safe, and creative environment in which to learn and experiment. The more you understand about what each partner in the process does, the more you will be able to get from class, and the more you can enjoy the process of learning new ways of moving.

Participating in a modern dance class is a great way to engage both your body and your mind.

Physical Environment

Depending on where you take dance class, your class may take place in a room that has many purposes or in a dedicated dance studio. It may be a fairly large room with metal or wooden railings, called barres, that are either attached to the walls or are portable and can stand alone. The room may have mirrors lining one wall. They are there to help your instructor see everyone in the room and for you and your instructor to see your form and alignment. While the mirrors may seem a little intimidating at first, you will quickly become accustomed to using them to learn. Usually dance studios have wooden or vinyl floors that give when you jump and land. Some dance classes are taught in gyms or auditoriums with no barres or mirrors.

> **SAFETY TIP** ▶▶▶▶▶▶▶▶▶▶▶▶▶▶▶▶▶▶▶▶▶▶▶
>
> Know the proper use of any equipment, including the barres, in the dance space before you use it. While barres look very sturdy, they are not intended to hold your full weight for climbing or hanging; they function only as aides for balancing.

Role of the Teacher

Dance teachers are emissaries of the art form. How your teacher views modern dance will influence how class is conducted and what ideas will be presented to you. The instructor's views can greatly influence your understanding of dance as an expressive and artistic medium.

One common perspective for teaching modern dance is that the students have a great deal of agency, or power, in determining what they learn. This means that it is the teacher's job not only to give the students new information but also to create opportunities for students to explore new ideas. This permits you to progress at your own rate. A more advanced student will not be held back by more inexperienced students in the class because each dancer will be learning at an appropriate level through personal experimentation.

You can expect that at some point in your modern dance class the teacher will give you feedback or constructive criticism on your dancing. This may be in the form of comments to the entire class or comments directed specifically to you. You can rest assured that the teacher will not give you any feedback on your execution that you won't be able to apply with practice. Many teachers wait until they know you and your movements well before giving any specific feedback. While there are certainly parameters related to form, alignment, aesthetics, and safety that will guide a teacher's feedback to students, there is no absolute right in modern dance. There are many successful ways to execute a movement if you are dancing artistically, not mechanically. The teacher, therefore, can give you expert feedback but not an absolute evaluation. The teacher's responsibility is to provide ideas with which you can explore and experiment and to guide you through your own learning. This is what is known as a **process-oriented approach**.

Role of the Musician

Many modern dance classes have live accompaniment. This can be a piano, drums, guitar, or combination of instruments. The musician is not merely a source of sound and rhythm to dance to. He is another artist in the class, creating inspiration and atmosphere. Musicians may play written music that fits the **tempo**, quality, and **meter** of the dance exercise, or they may improvise (spontaneously create music to go with what they see happening in class). By the way he plays or phrases the music, the accompanist will give the dancers cues about when movements change or cues to indicate when dancers should start moving. Listen carefully and you will feel the music supporting your dancing. The musician who plays for your class is a good resource for understanding the many connections between music and dance. The style of music he selects to accompany an exercise can give you information about the qualities of the movement itself. Do you hear a soft, lyrical sound? Do you hear a bright, crisp feel in the music? Dancing with your ears as well as your eyes can greatly enhance the artistry of your dancing. A good musician understands his responsibility to help you do this. Students assist him in this effort by not standing so as to block his view of the dancers.

Role of the Student

Students in modern dance have responsibilities toward themselves. The first is to participate as fully as possible. While some movements in modern dance may be unfamiliar, or the idea of improvising might seem embarrassing at first, very little progress can be made in technique without your full physical and mental participation. A key to this participation is observing the teacher as closely as possible and listening carefully to all instruction and imagery that may be given

Live music can inspire your dancing.

with a particular exercise. Thinking that you know how to do a step because you have had years of training and not listening carefully to the variation on the step that is being addressed in class are detrimental to your progress. Dancing the way you have danced before will only reinforce old techniques or perhaps bad habits. To progress, be open to the possibility that familiar steps can be done in new ways. Keep an open mind to new or unfamiliar ideas.

DID YOU KNOW? ▶▶▶▶▶▶▶▶▶

Dance and music are sister arts. The music in the modern dance class supports learning about movement and music while it enhances the classroom experience. Many modern dance classes have musicians who will create the music to match how you are dancing. Modern dance choreography can have original music, too. Many famous modern dancers, such as Martha Graham, considered composers to be among their most important collaborators in the creative process and had music created especially for their choreography.

EXPECTATIONS AND ETIQUETTE FOR STUDENTS

Like any social or school-related activity, dance classes have traditions and rules of conduct. These allow you to participate safely and cooperatively with others while facilitating a smoothly operating class. These traditions and rules include how and when to interact with the instructor, the musician, and other students and how to prepare for class.

Preparing and Practicing

You are expected to come to each class prepared, wearing appropriate attire. Preparation also includes practicing what you learned in the previous class session. Practice time during class is not enough for you to effectively learn movements or steps. You must set aside at least 15 minutes every day to practice new movements and combinations that you learned. During class, you must show respect for your teacher and classmates by not talking with other students and waiting until the instructor asks for questions. To better prepare for your next class, make mental notes or write down new steps for future practice, find after-class practice partners, and use any resources that your teacher provides. More suggestions for reflecting on class and improving in your practice time are included in the web resource for chapter 2. Most dance teachers are available after class or by appointment if you need extra instructions. Take advantage of any extra practice or rehearsal time. Video clips of positions or steps can be very effective while you are practicing.

Be patient with yourself! It takes time for the body to adjust to changes in routine and training. Part of this patience means finding perspective on your progress and shortcomings, so take the time to reflect on new information, skills, and perspectives. Corrections and feedback from the teacher are compliments. It should tell you not that the teacher thinks you did something wrong but that she thinks you have the potential to get better. Keeping this perspective and being patient with making changes in your technique will speed your progress as a dancer.

Attending Class Consistently

Missing classes means missing opportunities to learn, and it puts you behind in your development as a dancer. It may demonstrate the fact that you do not take the class or the teacher seriously. If you have to miss class, contact your teacher regarding skills you missed and find out how you can make up any practice times.

Arriving On Time

Some actions demonstrate disrespect to the class, your classmates, and the instructor. Arriving late to class is one such action. You should arrive to class at least 10 minutes early to mentally and physically prepare for class. Your teacher may provide you with some pre-warm-up activities to help you prepare for class.

Dressing Properly

Your attire shows your seriousness for learning in a technique class. Dance attire that covers the knees and abdomen is essential. Many modern dance classes will require you to move on your knees on the floor, so covering your knees with tights or pants will protect your skin. Although the dress codes in some private dance studios allow for more fashionable short-shorts or midriff-baring tops, the tradition in modern dance is to avoid that type of clothing. Similarly, fashion garments like scarves and jewelry are not acceptable and could even lead to injury if they became entangled in clothes and hair. Keep your hair secured away from your face. Each school will have its own policy for attire. Some require the students to wear specific styles of leotards and tights, or tights and T-shirts for men. Other schools allow for more personal choice. Your teacher will likely specify appropriate attire before your first class. Most modern dance classes require bare feet rather than footwear. Some instructors allow half shoes, or specially designed modern dance shoes, but traditional modern dance approaches hope to condition the skin on the soles of the feet so that wearing a modern shoe impedes this progress. Again, check with your teacher or school to determine the policy on footwear in class.

> **TECHNIQUE TIP** ▶▶▶▶▶▶▶▶▶▶
>
> Don't look to match yourself with other dancers in the class. There is no one type of body in modern dance that is best—other than a healthy one. Different styles of modern dance prefer different types of dancers both physically and artistically. Modern dance is not about shaping yourself to a mold; it is about finding your artistic voice through dance.

STRUCTURE OF MODERN DANCE CLASS

The structure of a modern dance technique class varies depending on the style of dance taught. The styles of modern dance are examined later in this book, but to give you an idea of what modern dance classes have in common in structure and content, an overview is provided here.

Each modern dance class consists of six elements. The order of these sections can vary, and some teachers may combine some elements into one section of class. In general, however, you should expect to participate in a warm-up, standing exercises, floor or seated exercises, exercises moving across the floor, movement combinations, and a cool-down.

Warm-Up

A dance class is structured so that it gradually warms up your body. Both the standing exercises and the seated exercises will prepare your body to do the more strenuous dance combinations at the end of class. Many dancers like to get themselves somewhat warm before the class so that they are prepared to dance the beginning class exercises even more fully. If you would like to do this kind of general warm-up, you would move continuously in active motions to increase your body temperature. The movements do not specifically need to be related to dance. Jogging or vigorous walking and joint rotations will get your heart rate slightly elevated and begin the process of raising your body temperature. A good warm-up should cause some sweating but not fatigue. Even just 5 minutes of this before a dance class will better prepare your body, especially if it is your first class of the day.

Standing Exercises

A good portion of a modern dance class takes place while standing in the center of the room. The exercises you do here build specific physical skills, coordination, and understanding of the aesthetics of the genre. These exercises include sequences of movements to articulate the feet, legs, back, and arms. Often coordination of these body parts is emphasized in this part of class. The way that movements are put together in the arms and legs varies from style to style in modern dance. You can learn the preferences of your instructor by paying attention to the way he puts together the exercises in this part of the class. For example, do the arms and legs work in opposition (right arm with the left leg)? Does the upper body often bend in the direction of the working leg or away from it? The answers to these questions and other observations you will make will help you get a feeling for the various styles of dance that fall under the term *modern dance*.

Floor or Seated Exercises

In some styles of modern dance, this is the first section of the class; in others it occurs later in the class. The exercises in this part of class are done while seated or lying on the studio floor. These exercises can emphasize coordination of body parts together without worrying about issues of balance or gravity. Often floor exercises are meant to develop flexibility or core strength. Floor exercises are also important as a way to explore the idea of weightedness, which is a central concept in modern dance. Learning to yield to gravity, push into the floor, and use the

The floor is a source of energy and a partner in your modern dance training.

floor surface as a partner in creating or executing movement can all be developed in this section of class.

Movements Across the Floor

After you are sufficiently warmed up through the standing and seated exercises, you will learn movement sequences that travel through the space of the studio, either from one side of the room to the other or from one corner of the room to the opposite corner. There are two goals of this section of class. The first is to learn **locomotor** skills. These are movements that travel through space, such as stylized walking or running, skipping, hopping, galloping, sliding, jumping, leaping, or turning. The second goal of this part of the class is to put sequences of traveling movements together. Dancers take turns during this section of class, usually with two, three, or four dancers at a time (depending on the size of the class) traveling across the floor at the same time. Movements in this section are generally done from both the right and left sides of the room so that you can learn to complete the movements on both the left and right foot.

Movement Combinations

Most modern dance classes end with a movement combination. This is where your teacher puts together a small dance. It can be created from other movements you learned in class that day, or it can be new material. The length of the dance varies according to the teacher, but it is often long enough so that you can work on your skill of remembering movement sequences. Some combinations travel across the space; others take place in the center of the floor. Sometimes combinations will be started in one class and finished or added to during successive classes. If the school where you take classes ends the term with an informal showing of dances, this is the time in class where you will most likely work on that material.

Cool-Down

Most modern dance classes end with a brief closing exercise. Sometimes this is a movement sequence that stretches your legs; sometimes it consists of slow movements that return your heart rate and breathing to normal after a vigorous combination. Some instructors have their students make a circle for closing remarks or reflections. There is often applause at the end of the cool-down portion of class. If you have a musician in your class, it is appropriate to direct some of the applause to the musician as well as to the teacher.

UNIQUE FEATURES OF MODERN DANCE

Five features of a modern dance class are distinct from features of other styles of dance: emphasis on floor movements, use of improvisation alongside structured movement, use of both curved and straight spine, incorporation of turned-out and parallel legs, and use of both flexed and pointed feet. Each style of modern dance, and each teacher within that style, will emphasize these unique features of modern dance differently. These choices are referred to as the aesthetic preferences, or artistic qualities, of each style of modern dance. The specifics of the differences between five major styles of modern dance are covered in depth in chapter 8, but in general, modern dance classes have the following features in common.

Floor Movement

The aesthetics of modern dance often use the floor in choreography. Movements that fall to the floor as well as movements that stay on the floor are often seen in modern dance where the floor represents a valid, usable part of the stage for choreography. Some styles of modern dance see the earth as representing the source of energy and strength for the dancer; others see it as symbolic of giving in, or surrendering to, the power of gravity. In either case, much choreography revolves around its use.

Improvised or Interpreted Movement

Improvisation in a modern dance class means asking the dancers to create movements of their own invention. Often this can be a few counts of movement inside of or at the end or beginning of a phrase of choreography that has been taught by the instructor. This can be a separate section of class or incorporated into one or more of the sections of class already described. Not all modern teachers include improvisation in their classes. If they do, this is a good opportunity to tune in to your own artistic voice. The intent is to learn to respond in the moment to the impulses you feel from the music or the images given in the instructions for the improvisation and express them through movement. This personal response is an important part of the modern dance class. It's a chance for you to build your own artistic repertoire of movement. Just as the founders of modern dance sought new ways to express themselves, as a current modern dancer you are being encouraged to do the same. Find your voice by listening to your inner impulses.

Many forms of modern dance incorporate the use of improvisation as a way to create choreography; others use it as a style of performance. This means that in some forms of modern dance the movements of the performance are not set; they are created each time a performance takes place. The guidelines for these performances are still rehearsed, and the dancers are given only a certain amount of latitude in the kind of movements that are allowed. In other instances, the dancers improvise under direction of the choreographer, who shapes their movements and creates a piece of set choreography that includes the dancers' movement inventions. In either case, the ability to create movement may be a skill that is valued in a modern dance class.

Use of the Spine

Many styles of modern dance create a lot of movements that begin in the center of the torso. The preferred movements in modern dance include both a straight spine and a curved or twisted line. This means that modern dance classes will focus on the articulation of the spine so that dancers can learn to shape the torso in a variety of directions as needed by the choreographer.

Parallel and Turned-Out Positions

This refers to using turned-out legs and also working with the feet and hips facing forward, a position known as parallel. More detail on the differences between these is discussed in chapter 4.

Pointed and Flexed Feet

Both flexed feet and pointed feet are used in the modern dance movement vocabulary. A flexed foot is one in which the toes face upward, causing the ankle to flex at a 90-degree angle. A pointed foot is one in which the toes are extended forward. Your teacher will clarify which kind of foot articulation you need to use.

APPRECIATING MODERN DANCE AS A PERFORMING ART

To get the most from your technique classes, as in any class you take, you need to understand the context of the information you are learning. In other words, what is the big picture? How do the things that you are learning in technique class connect with the art of dance as it is practiced by professionals or by dancers all over the world? The best way to come to an understanding of this context is to see a performance by a professional modern dance company. Most major cities have theaters where modern dance is being performed by both local and national companies on tour. If you do not live in an area where modern dance is performed regularly, there are many excellent video recordings available. The web resource that accompanies this textbook has links to resources where you can find examples of professional modern dance. The more choreographers you can see, the better your understanding of the art of modern dance will be. These experiences will help you to see not only the great variety of dance in this genre but also the qualities that modern dance performances have in common. It can also help you to see the variety of body types that make up the professional modern dance world and how a professional choreographer can use articulate, trained bodies to create this art form. Live dance performances and professional dance videos are also excellent material on which to reflect in your dance journal. More guidance on viewing dance and dance journaling is presented in chapter 6 and the web resource for chapter 2.

SUMMARY

Modern dance refers to several styles of dance that began in the early 20th century during an era of rebellion and change. These styles, many of which come directly from historical figures in dance, have in common the use of the floor, articulation of the torso, the use of breath, and often improvisation. Today's modern dance often involves a fusion of movement vocabularies. Studying modern dance can help you mentally, emotionally, and physically as you learn to find your own artistic voice and express who you are through movement. This is a skill dancers work on throughout their lives. Certain rules of behavior will be expected of you in a modern dance technique class, including wearing the appropriate clothing and being respectful of the teacher, musician, and other students. You can expect to participate in standing exercises, floor exercises, across-the-floor movements, movement combinations, and a cool-down.

To find supplementary materials for this chapter, such as learning activities, e-journal assignments, and web links, visit the web resource at **www.HumanKinetics.com/BeginningModernDance1E.**

Chapter 2

Preparing for Class

Learning a new art form is an exciting time in your education. By taking a modern dance class, you have the opportunity to express yourself in a new way and explore a world of movement that connects you to some of the most innovative artists of the 20th and 21st centuries. To maximize your modern dance class experience, you will need to be prepared both bodily and intellectually. This chapter outlines steps for physical and mental preparation and ideas for enhancing the development of new skills. These preparations include learning how to guide your own journey in modern dance so that you make the most of the experience.

DRESSING FOR CLASS

The traditional attire for a modern dance class is a leotard and tights with bare feet, although many studios and schools allow for close-fitting exercise clothing such as yoga pants or tank tops. In many classes, students are free to select their own attire, although it is common for schools or teachers to have a dress code. So be sure to ask your instructor what the expectation is for your class. Women can find dance or sport bras at many dance or sport retail stores. Dance belts are recommended for men. Similar to jock straps, dance belts are designed especially for dance. They protect genitals, and they eliminate visible lines under tights.

Regardless of what you wear, allow for proper fit, support, comfort, and ample freedom of movement. Before class, remove jewelry to ensure safety for your jewelry, yourself, and other dancers. Also for safety reasons, pull your hair back and secure it away from the face, even if your hair is short. There are several styles of half shoes, or modern dance shoes, but these are not necessary for participation in a modern dance class. Some dancers like these shoes because they facilitate turning; some instructors prohibit them because they inhibit connection with the floor. Again, ask your instructor about footwear as well as attire to ensure you are well prepared.

These students are properly dressed for class with comfortable, well-fitting clothing and with hair pulled back.

CARRYING DANCE GEAR

Use a dance bag to carry your clothes, shoes, and other items to and from class. You can find bags designed specifically for dance gear at dance apparel stores and online, but gym bags work well, too. Bags can become heavy when they contain a collection of stuff you rarely need or use, so make wise choices about what you need for before and after class. Items to consider include the following:

- Towel
- Deodorant
- Adhesive bandages or specially designed foot tape available at hospital supply stores
- Hair clips, pins, ponytail holders, hairnets, and headbands
- A tennis ball or fitness band to aid in stretching

- A separate bag for wet or used practice clothing
- Personal grooming items and extra towel if you plan to shower after class
- Water bottle and light snack for after class
- Journal book or other supplies for writing notes after class

After class, it is easy to dump your wet dance clothes and shoes into your dance bag, zip it, and go. If your class is early in the day or the weather is warm, separate your damp practice clothes from your shoes and other items in your dance bag. Remove the damp items, air out your shoes, and leave your dance bag open before packing for your next dance class.

PREPARING YOURSELF MENTALLY AND PHYSICALLY

Dressing for class helps you attain the appearance of a dancer, but it is only part of preparing for class; you also need mental and physical preparation. To give yourself adequate time to prepare your mind and body for class, make a habit of arriving to the studio early.

Physical Preparation

Since a modern dance class involves physical activity, it is a good idea to warm up your body immediately before the start of the class. Most dance classes will begin gently so that your body can acclimate to larger movements, but it is still valuable to be physically ready before the class starts. To prepare the muscles for the demands that will be placed on them in class, you need to have good blood circulation. The blood provides the muscles with the oxygen necessary to flex and contract. You will want to get your circulation going with some walking, jogging in place, or other mild aerobic activity. The muscles will also need glycogen, or blood sugar, to operate. This means you will need to have some food and water in your system for class. Chapter 3 goes into specific detail about the nutritional needs of dancers, but in general, be sure you have not eaten immediately before class, because this may cause stomach cramps. But do not go to class hungry. You risk damaging your muscles by dancing with insufficient fuel. Bring water with you for drinking during class, but save sport drinks for after dancing.

The usual practice is to arrive to the studio 20 minutes before the start of class, if your schedule allows. You can address items 1 and 4 can at another time if scheduling is tight, but you should allow some mental and physical preparation time before class begins. About 20 minutes of lead time will allow you to do the following:

1. Five minutes to change into the appropriate attire for class. In most places this will include stowing your dance bag in a locker or dressing room. It is best not to bring bags with you into the studio. Make sure that your cell phone is turned off so that it does not interrupt class. Street shoes are not allowed on a dance studio floor, so be sure to remove them when going to the dressing room.

2. Five minutes of light aerobic activity, such as jogging or walking to increase blood flow.

3. Five minutes for working on stretching or a specific skill that you will focus on in class, recalling the combination if that will be repeated or added on to, and assessing how your body feels. During this time, ask yourself if you have any injuries you should be cautious of in class or make the teacher aware of. This is also a good time to remind yourself of the specific goals you want to work on in the class.

4. Five minutes for socializing and getting to know your fellow dancers. After all, dance is also about building an artistic community, and communication between dancers is necessary for establishing this.

Modern dance is a wonderful physical activity that can improve physical fitness. Physical fitness can be related to motor skills or to health. **Health-related fitness components** that can be enhanced by dance are muscular strength and endurance, flexibility, and body composition. **Skill-related fitness components** consist of coordination, agility, balance, power, reaction time, and speed.

Muscular Strength and Endurance

Muscular strength is the ability of the muscle to exert maximal force against a resistance, whereas **muscular endurance** is the ability of the muscle to keep repeating force over time. Modern dance improves muscular endurance by forcing muscles to do repeated contractions. This can improve muscle tone, tendon and ligament strength, and bone density, which lead to increased muscular strength.

Flexibility

Flexibility is the ability of the joint to move freely through the full range of motion. Flexibility is important in modern dance because it gives you a larger range of motion, so flexibility exercises are often included in class. Muscles have elastic properties and respond to stretching by temporarily lengthening. Although joint capsules, ligaments, and tendons are not elastic, with proper stretching they can permanently lengthen and increase in range of motion. Maintaining an appropriate range of motion in joints enhances quality of life and improves dance technique. Always use proper technique when stretching any muscle so as not to overstretch to the point of injury.

Body Composition

Body composition consists of the muscle, fat, bone, and other tissues that make up the total weight of a person. In the past, doctors and trainers used height-and-weight charts to determine recommended body weight for optimal health. However, determining how much of the total body weight is fat can give people a more realistic and healthy target for body weight. Body composition can be determined through hydrostatic (underwater) weight, skinfold thickness, girth measurement, bioelectrical impedance, and air displacement. To determine your body composition, seek the help of a professional. The more you are involved in physical activity, such as dance, the more your body composition can reach a healthy level.

Skill-Related Fitness

Modern dance requires successful motor performance. With practice, these skills can be improved:

Agility is the ability to change body positions and directions.

Balance is the ability to maintain the body in proper equilibrium.

Coordination is the integration of nervous and muscular systems to perform harmonious body movements.

Power is the ability to produce maximum force in a short time.

Reaction time is the time required to initiate a response to a stimulus.

Speed is the ability to propel the body from one place to another.

In addition to the physical preparation necessary for studying modern dance, you need to be prepared mentally for class.

Mental Preparation

While it might be technically possible to work your body without considering the mental side of dancing, this will not train you to be a dancer. This is in part what separates dance from recreational exercise. You can participate in an aerobics class by watching and following, and as long as you ensure the alignment of your body for safety, you will have a good class. This is not true of dance. Rather than move as the teacher does, you need to consider how it feels for your body, which may be very different from the way the teacher or your fellow dancers experience the movement. In many ways you are your own teacher in a dance class. You are the only expert on what it feels like to do the movements you are doing, or what emotions are evoked when you dance fully. One of the things that makes dance an art form is the difference in your inner experiences. You have a unique way of appreciating your body in motion. Getting in touch with your uniqueness is the beginning of developing an artistic voice through dance. The teacher scaffolds the experience to provide valuable ideas to investigate and a safe atmosphere for accomplishing this.

Getting yourself in the habit of being mentally aware in dance class can lead to advances as a performer, too. If you have trained yourself through class to be aware of how you are moving, you will be able to think about more that just the sequence of steps when you perform. You will have developed the

DID YOU KNOW? ▶▶▶▶▶▶▶▶

It is the dancer's responsibility to engage in a mental exploration of the concepts in class. Watching and repeating do not make a dancer. Watching, repeating, exploring, and evaluating do.

mental stamina to think beyond just the sequence and to concentrate on the quality of movement and the depth of character that you are portraying. Habits developed in technique class will be reflected in your performing experiences. One way to develop this mental focus is to dance mindfully. The next section of this chapter explains the concept of mindfulness and how you can apply it to dance class.

Dancing Mindfully

Have you ever had the experience of traveling to a place to which you have driven many times, only to find yourself at a traffic light halfway to your destination where you "wake up" and say to yourself, "How did I get this far? I don't really remember driving all this way!" This is an example of **mindlessness**. If there had been a major traffic jam or road closing, the new information would have startled you into paying attention to these behaviors to which you are so familiar. Paying more attention to things that have become rote habits is called **mindfulness**.

A mindful approach to new experiences allows the brain to absorb more information and to make fuller use of the information gained. Most important, an openness in thinking allows for the possibility of change in behavior because it moves you away from automatic response patterns.

> ### DID YOU KNOW? ▶ ▶ ▶ ▶ ▶ ▶ ▶ ▶
>
> The term *mindfulness* was developed by Harvard psychologist Ellen Langer in her 1989 book of the same title.

Mindlessness can seriously stifle your growth and success as a dancer. If every time you are confronted with a familiar movement and you approach it in the same way, there is no room for development or innovation. For example, the dance teacher gives you an exercise. You immediately recognize it as the same that was assigned yesterday and say to yourself, "Okay, I know this exercise. Let's begin. I know what to do." You will repeat the exercise mostly the way you did it the day before, adding to your experience only the benefit of repetition. Let's add to the example the idea that the instructor gave you some feedback or correction on your exercise the day before, so now your mind might say, "Okay, this is the exercise where the teacher told me I am gripping with my quadriceps too much. I need to relax them more today." Now a familiar exercise is seen as an opportunity to reach for a new goal or to make technical progress. Even without the instructor's comment, you could look at the familiar movement sequence and say, "Okay, since I have done this exercise before, I don't have to worry about this sequence too much. I can work on my personal goal of dancing more musically and fluidly." Mindfulness means approaching every exercise as if you have been given a new focus or goal every time you attempt it. It is a frame of mind from which you can learn no matter what kind of class you are taking. It puts the responsibility for growth on you rather than on the teacher. It is up to you as a dancer to push yourself to develop as an artist. The instructor is there to guide you, inform you, inspire you, and enrich you—but only you can refresh your perspective, enliven your mind, and take charge of going as far as you can with your dancing.

Modern dance teachers give individual feedback to encourage you and ensure proper technique.

Charting Your Own Course

Perhaps the most challenging task you have as a beginning student in a modern dance class is understanding the responsibility you have for guiding your own progress. The teacher is your leader by providing you with ideas worthy of investigation and the physical and mental tools for these explorations. It is your job, however, to respond fully and artistically to the material given in class. It is fun to take class, and often dancers just want to come into the studio and move for their own enjoyment. This is a perfectly valid reason to take class, and some days this may be exactly what your mind and body need. If, however, this is the only attitude you bring to your modern dance class, you will be following a path of entertainment and not education and may limit the possibilities of what you can learn through dance technique class.

To make the most of class, you will need to put in your mind and your spirit alongside your bodily participation. Use your brain in class! Rather than focusing only on the sequence of dance moves given to you, focus on the quality of the movement. The teacher is less concerned that you know which steps follow the others and more concerned about how you are doing the steps. Are you moving sharply when required? Are you paying attention to the transitions between steps? Are you focusing your gaze in places other than the mirror? You and the instructor will work together to determine what skills you will focus on for the semester or term. It will, in part, be up to you to ensure that you stay focused on these goals while you are taking class.

Habits can be hard to break, and if you are in the habit of doing what you are already good at, progress will be hard to achieve. It feels good to do the steps that you do well, but if you are a serious student, you will give equal focus to repeating steps that you find challenging. There is a great personal satisfaction in working hard to achieve something you find difficult to do and then meeting your goal. Don't deprive yourself of this fulfillment by working only on skills you find easier to accomplish. This kind of long-term goal setting requires delayed gratification. You have to be willing to be patient with yourself and not expect that every aspect of dance will come easily to you. You have unique challenges and strengths. Simply because a step is difficult for others does not mean it will be difficult for you. Conversely, some things that come easily to your classmates may present a challenge for you. Do not be discouraged. Master choreographer Martha Graham said it takes 10 years to become a dancer. This is definitely a goal worth working on!

The four essential steps to ensuring that you develop your skills as a modern dancer are reflection, repetition, artistry, and patience. These habits will help you to improve your dancing, recognize your progress, and find satisfaction in expressing yourself through movement.

Reflection   To stay focused on your goals—both the small ones that you are working on daily in class and the larger ones that you want to accomplish over time—you need to think about your own progress. This is called reflection. Reflection involves thinking about what you want to accomplish, what you have done so far, and what feedback you have received from your teacher in class. It involves a daily review of your dance experiences as a habit. This means once you leave the studio you spend some concentrated time each day reviewing what was learned in class. Just the simple act of thinking about the class will help you to retain information you were given and focus your energy for the next class.

Repetition   The second essential step is repetition. Habits in both the body and the mind are not formed until there is lots of repetition. You may think that you have done an exercise before or that you already know a step well, but the act of repeating movements builds a critical foundation in your body. Repetition in good form builds physical strength and stamina. This is similar to athletes who run drills to build these qualities. Repetition of the foundations also helps to prevent injury by building habits that ensure proper form and therefore not strain you. Many dancers, especially those new to a particular technique, like to say, "But we did that before!" Try to change your mental response to "Good—something familiar that will give me the chance to really get this to be automatic in my body!" If an instructor repeats a particular skill or exercise frequently, it is because he thinks it is important to your development as a dancer or your understanding of that style of modern dance. You need to know movements, alignment, transitional steps, shapes, and rhythms so well that you can execute them without a lot of mental work. This frees up your mind to pay attention to the quality of the movements you are doing. Are you performing the exercise fluidly, for example, or in the character that the choreography demands? If you have not repeated a movement enough, you will need to expend mental energy on the details of execution and will not be able to move into the artistic phase of your performance.

Artistry   Whenever possible, pay attention to the *how* of your dancing. This is the artistic step. Although it is difficult, especially for dancers new to modern dance, to let go of focusing on which step comes next, it is vital for your development as a dancer to begin thinking about how you are executing steps. When a teacher demonstrates a movement, try to notice how she is performing the movements as well as what she is doing. A guide for looking at dance for its qualities comes later in this book, but in the meantime, ask yourself some basic questions:

- Which part of the body is the most important in this movement?
- Are the legs, arms, and torso moving together or as separate units?
- Is the movement sharp or smooth?
- Does the movement look like it is heavy (is the pull of gravity obvious), or does the body seem to float in the air?
- Is the movement done quickly, or is there a sense of continuity?
- Does the movement cover a lot of space in the room?
- Does this movement match the music in some way?

Thinking about these elements is the first step to dancing artistically. It will develop the mental habit of focusing on both how and what you are dancing, which are essential skills for any performer. The more you can practice tuning in to these elements during technique class, the easier it will be to tune in to them in an audition. This will separate you from the other dancers who are solely focused on which step comes next. Making minor mistakes in sequence is less important. Of course, it will be essential to develop the ability to pick up steps quickly and correctly, but the mental habits you develop in technique class of learning to pick up how artistically the movement should be executed while picking up the sequence will lead to success.

Patience   The final essential step is perhaps the most difficult. Be patient! Any art form worth learning takes time and patience. You need to be patient with yourself in developing your skills through repetition. This is not a process that can be hurried. Your body and mind need time to absorb and integrate the information you are learning in technique class. Everyone learns at a different speed. Be careful not to compare yourself to the dancer next to you, but stay focused on doing what you need to do to improve. This can be hard advice to follow, especially if your progress is not what you expected. Many dancers who are used to picking things up quickly or being at the top of their class academically can be frustrated if they don't sense that their bodies are progressing as quickly as they'd like. You can't expect your progress to always be a steady upward slope. Sometimes your learning landscape hits a plateau. This doesn't mean you aren't making progress simply because you need to keep practicing. It is that practice and repetition that will allow you to cross the plateau to the next upward slope of obvious improvement. Crossing the plateau is progress—it just looks different than what you are accustomed to seeing as improvement. Accepting some delayed gratification of your goals is a part of developing as an artist and a dancer.

Mind–Body Preparation

Your mind and body are not separate parts of your being. Your body responds to your thinking, and your mind is informed about the world around you by the sensory stimulation that your body provides. Modern dance can help you to understand this mind–body connection even more clearly by developing your spatial and kinesthetic senses and your ability to recognize movement patterns.

Gaining Spatial Sense

Through modern dance class you will develop the ability to tell where your body is with respect to the dance space and how your body parts are positioned with respect to one another. This is called **spatial sense**. Body directions are more complex than simply front, side, and back, and these directions change as you move through space. Each part of your body has many possible positions in space. As you learn the movement vocabulary, or the steps, shapes, and movements of modern dance, you will also develop your sense of the space around you.

Developing Your Kinesthetic Sense

In addition to being able to sense yourself in the space, taking modern dance classes will help you to develop an awareness of how your body moves as you imitate movements you see or imagine new ones. Your ability to see a movement and replicate it on your own body, or to imagine a movement and represent that idea in your body, is known as your **kinesthetic sense**. This idea is sometimes called **proprioception** in medical terms. It is how your body translates what you see, hear, and imagine into the way your body moves. Dance classes of all kinds will help you to hone this sense.

Seeing Movement Patterns

When you keenly observe movements in class, you can recognize patterns in them. This helps you to memorize movement sequences. Just like when you learned to read, you first learned to recognize individual letters, then syllables, and then whole words. When you start taking modern dance classes, you may recognize only individual movements, but soon patterns of shapes and combinations of movements will become familiar to you.

SUMMARY

In this chapter you have learned that you will need to prepare physically and mentally to get the most from your modern dance class. If you do prepare, you can develop many skills through modern dance, such as spatial and kinesthetic sense and the physical skills of improved agility, balance, coordination, and muscular strength and endurance. As a student, you are responsible for helping to guide your own journey by reflecting on what you have learned and by dancing with a mindful attitude. This means that you will need to be aware of the expectations in the class and not relax into old habits. If you prepare both mentally and physically for your modern dance classes, you will get much more out of them than just a period of exercise. You will see how modern dance can nurture your mind, body, and spirit.

To find supplementary materials for this chapter, such as learning activities, e-journal assignments, and web links, visit the web resource at **www.HumanKinetics.com/BeginningModernDance1E.**

Chapter 3

Safety and Health

Whether you are an experienced dancer or new to dance classes, you will need to know how to keep yourself safe and healthy in the dance studio. Since your body is your artistic medium as a dancer, it is especially important to understand how to care for your body to prevent injury and keep it in the best possible shape for performance. This chapter covers basic information on studio safety, injury prevention, anatomy, flexibility, fitness, and nutrition, all of which are tools for maintaining and lengthening your life as a dancer.

STUDIO SAFETY

The dance studio is a safe environment in which to learn and develop. Some practices, however, will aid your studio experience. Most dance studios have rules to ensure safety for all dancers and for the studio facility itself. Where modern dance is concerned, these usually relate to respecting the space of the studio itself through what you do—or more accurately do not—wear or bring to class.

Equipment and Storage

Many dance studios have equipment for use in classes, such as portable or stationary ballet barres, elastic bands for resistance work, fitness or yoga mats, and sound systems. It is important for your own safety not to use equipment outside of supervised uses with an instructor. Returning equipment carefully after use will also ensure the durability of the equipment and the safety of the next user.

Another way to respect the physical space of the studio is to help keep it clean by not bringing any food or drinks other than water into the space. Ask your instructor if water bottles are allowed in the studio. Chewing gum is prohibited in dance studios for the safety of the dancers and also to keep the space sanitary. The studio is the heart of a dance program. You will spend a lot of hours in the studio and you will want it to be well cared for.

Floors

Modern dance classes include portions in which you will need to move on the floor, so the surface needs to be clean. Some modern dance classes allow dancers to wear half sandals specially made for modern dance classes, but these are never worn outside the studio, so they shouldn't affect the cleanliness of the space. Street shoes are never permitted in a dance studio.

You may be surprised to know that elements of what you wear, such as lotions or creams that you put on your skin or hair, can cause serious safety issues during a dance class. These creams transfer onto the floor during floor work when you are lying down and can create an invisible slippery space that can cause injury to you or other dancers in the class. It is best to avoid using these immediately before class. Similarly, certain kinds of toenail polish can transfer and mark a dance floor, especially if it is vinyl, if you are dancing barefoot, as is most common in modern class. Any hairpins or clips should be completely secured so they do not pose a hazard to nearby dancers if they come loose during quick or strenuous movement sequences. Similarly, wearing large earrings or bracelets and necklaces of any kind can cause injury to you or a dancer near you, so you should not wear these during class.

PERSONAL SAFETY

Dance is a safe activity, and the instructor and administration have policies to ensure that you do not harm yourself. This doesn't mean that dancers don't also have to take responsibility for keeping themselves healthy, though. Listen to your body and pace yourself as you begin to study modern dance.

The exercises in modern dance classes are intended to improve very specific physical skills. The muscles you use and the way that you use them in these classes may be entirely different than your previous training in dance or in other athletic activities. The choreography that you will have an opportunity to be a part of, the kinds of modern dance that you may experience, and the styles of the instructors that you encounter in modern dance will all put new demands on your physical and mental capabilities.

If you are a student who can be characterized as an overachiever (as so many dancers are!), then you may have a tendency to set unrealistically high expectations for yourself. Allow yourself time to get adjusted to your new routine and develop a fresh set of goals. Most people's peak performance and achievement come when they can concentrate and are not overly stressed. You may need to modify your expectations or the timetable for meeting your goals so that you can learn new information without additional stress. Learning new things in a new environment is stress enough!

Personal Space

Understanding your requirements for **personal space** during each section of the class is critical to your safety and enjoyment as well as the safety and enjoyment of your classmates. This means you should leave space around you to accommodate leg, arm, and body extensions without entering your neighbors' area. Your personal space surrounds you as you stand in one spot and as you move through the studio individually or in groups.

ACTIVITY ▶▶▶▶▶▶ ▶ ▶▶▶▶▶

Determining Your Personal Space

Stand in a place that has no barriers to movement. Extend your arms overhead, then out to the sides of your body. Extend each leg forward, then to the side and to the back. Finally, turn yourself around. You have outlined a somewhat spherical space, which is the amount of space you will need to execute movements in place. Think about moving within your sphere in relation to other students when moving in side-to-side and forward-and-back patterns in the middle of the studio or when moving in groups of two or three in a line across the floor or on a diagonal.

Dancers spread out across the studio in their personal space.

Personal Health Information

Personal health information is just that—personal information. If you have had an injury, surgery, or chronic health condition that might affect your physical performance or the health of your peers, you are not obligated to tell everyone, but you should tell your instructor. To protect privacy, usually instructors encourage students to see them after the first class. Your instructor should be aware of any chronic condition or disease such as asthma, diabetes, or epilepsy in order to be prepared for a possible emergency and also to help you to dance safely. If the instructor doesn't know your specific health conditions, it will be difficult for her to accommodate your needs.

BASIC ANATOMY

Anatomy is the study of the physical structures of the body, and **kinesiology** is the study of the body in motion. Often these two subjects are combined and are referred to as the study of **dynamic anatomy**. Dance is an art form that applies scientific principles of proper functioning to the human body. If you were a violinist, you would need to learn how to maintain your instrument and how to keep it functioning. You would need to learn to change the strings, apply rosin to the bow, and keep your instrument in tune in order to perform at a high level. Dance is no different. A dancer needs to learn the basic physical structures of the body and how they work together to create the movement options that a choreographer uses as an expressive artistic medium. This portion of the chapter offers some basic information on the structures of your body, which may help you to avoid injury and better understand the feedback you get from your teachers.

Skeletal System

Basic anatomy for dancers can be divided into understanding the bone structures of the body, or the skeleton, and understanding the muscular structures of the body. Figure 3.1 shows the bones that you will need to know from the front and back.

From time to time your dance instructor may refer to the bones involved in a particular exercise. This will be especially true when she is talking about proper alignment. Correct skeletal **alignment** occurs when weight is transferred through the center of each joint. This is the safest way for the body to move. Figure 3.2 shows a dancer in proper alignment. Most often when dance teachers talk about ensuring you are in proper alignment,

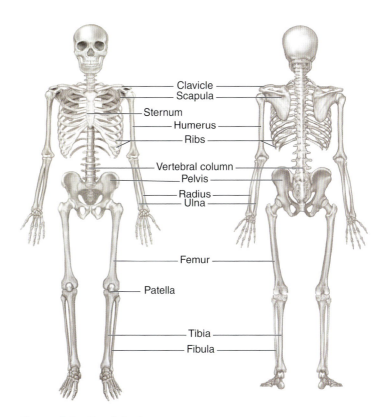

Figure 3.1 The skeletal system.

they are referring to skeletal alignment. When you are dancing, no matter what position your dancing takes you into, you will still need to be aware of how your bones are positioned so that you can dance safely and efficiently. For example, good spinal alignment when you are dancing means that your shoulders will be lined up over your hips, usually with the ribs gently hanging in between. Similarly, for leg alignment, your knees will be lined up with the center of your feet as you jump and travel through space.

Alignment is important not only for your bones but also for your muscles. When your skeleton is well aligned, your muscles can work at peak efficiency for the longest duration and with the least risk of injury. The body is a closed system. If you have misaligned the bones in one part of the body, then another part of the

Figure 3.2 Proper alignment.

body must compensate for that misalignment. This can lead to the unnecessary expenditure of muscle energy, tiring you quickly. Worse yet, it can be a recipe for injury. Proper alignment is a principle of all types and styles of dance.

Muscular System

Frequently you will hear your dance teacher refer to a specific muscle that is doing the work in a particular exercise. While it isn't practical or necessary to become an expert on every muscle of the body, it is extremely valuable to understand the basic muscular systems in your body. The more you can visualize what is happening inside your body as you dance, the more deeply you will understand how to use the phenomenal resources you have in your body. This will also aid your understanding of executing many movements and articulating what is happening in your body should injury occur. When you understand the muscles that you should be using and how to properly activate these muscles, you automatically improve your alignment and efficiency of movement. And in turn, this automatically decreases compensatory strategies and therefore decreases the risk of injury. Naturally the skeleton and muscles work together since the muscles are attached to the bones through connective tissue (ligaments and tendons). Understanding both and how they interact is important because in static standing, the alignment can appear correct; once movement occurs, alignment can be disrupted due to recruitment of incorrect muscles. Figure 3.3 shows the basic muscular systems of the body.

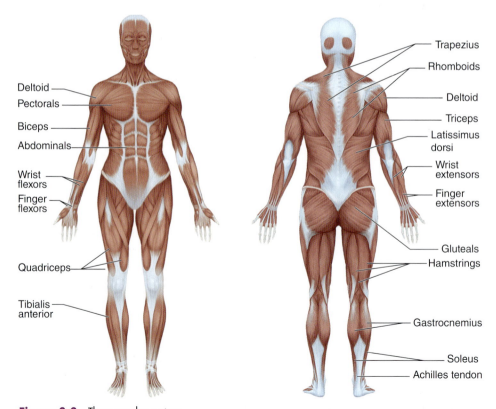

Figure 3.3 The muscular system.

In general, a muscle can do three types of actions. A muscle can shorten as it exerts force. This is called **concentric muscle action** (figure 3.4). A muscle can also lengthen as it exerts force. This is called **eccentric muscle action** (figure 3.4). And a muscle can neither lengthen nor shorten as force is exerted. This is called **isometric muscle action.** Muscles also have the remarkable ability to work in pairs. When one muscle in a pair contracts, or shortens, then the other muscle in the pair relaxes and lengthens. The contracting muscle is the **agonist** and the relaxing muscle is the **antagonist**. As you are seated reading this, tense the front of your thigh, the large muscle called the quadriceps (or quads). You can note that this causes the muscles in the back of your thigh, or the hamstrings, to relax. Your dance teacher has probably told you to relax your quads when you go to do a high kick in front of you. To get your leg fully extended in front of you, you will need the muscles of the hamstrings to push upward and the muscles deep in the side of the hip (the hip external rotators) to rotate outward. If you overtense the front of your thigh, the muscles in the back of your leg and side of the hip will relax and be unable to help you achieve this. Being aware of how your muscles function will help you to develop safe habits as you execute increasingly difficult movements. A muscle pair should be balanced in strength and flexibility to function effectively. Overdeveloping one muscle in a pair can also lead to injury or an inability to perform to your best ability.

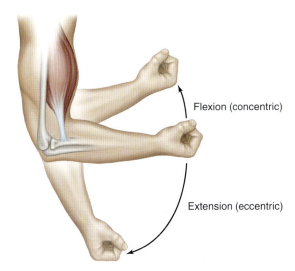

Flexion (concentric)

Extension (eccentric)

Figure 3.4 Muscle contractions: concentric and eccentric.

BASIC KINESIOLOGY

More dance injuries result from overload and biomechanical factors rather than from acute trauma (Clippinger 2007). Understanding basic kinesiology, or human movement, can help heal or prevent dance injuries. This section explains terms that relate to movement. Dancers and other athletes need to understand these terms in order to better communicate injuries or concerns with physicians, physical therapists, athletic trainers, or massage therapists. Also, understanding how the body moves in proper terms will make you a more informed dancer.

Anatomical Position

In addition to words like *bones*, *skeleton*, and *muscle*, which are part of your everyday vocabulary, there are some specific anatomical terms that may be helpful to you in understanding the workings of your artistic instrument, your body. The front of the body is referred to as the **anterior**, and the back of the body is referred to as the

posterior. The parts closest to the midline of your body are referred to as **medial**, and the parts farthest from the midline are referred to as **lateral**. This is just a way for scientists to map the body, a sort of north–south–east–west compass to your body. This also helps health professionals be specific. Is the pain in your knee medial (on the inside part), or is it posterior (in the back of the knee)? It also helps to create landmarks on the body. Even when your leg is turned out so that the front of your knee is facing to the side, this is still the anterior portion of the knee, no matter where in space it may be facing.

To understand movement, you must first understand basic anatomical terminology. The universal starting position used to describe movement is called the **anatomical position** (figure 3.5). It is an erect standing position with the feet forward, the arms down by the sides, and the palms forward with the thumbs pointing outward and fingers extended. The **prone** position is lying facedown on the front, and the **supine** position is lying faceup on the back.

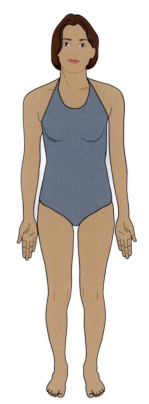

Figure 3.5 Anatomical position.

Connective Tissue

People often think of the muscles as being attached to bones, but in fact there is a complex system of connective tissue that actually serves this function. The body contains **ligaments,** which attach bones to other bones, and **tendons,** which attach muscles to bones. Both of these kinds of connective tissue—and many more that also exist in the body—are key to gaining flexibility, developing strength, maintaining stability, and executing clear and safe dance movements.

Joint Movements

Synovial joints permit these basic joint movements: **flexion** (decreasing joint angle, such as bending the elbow), **extension** (increasing joint angle, such as straightening the elbow; figure 3.6*a*), **hyperextension** (extending past natural position, such as bending backward), **abduction** (moving away from the midline), **adduction** (moving toward the midline; figure 3.6*b*), **rotation** (external, or turning the anterior surface outward, and internal, or turning anterior surface inward), and **circumduction** (movement that creates a complete circle and combines flexion, abduction, extension, and adduction; figure 3.6*c*).

Joint stability is the ability of a joint to withstand mechanical shocks or movements without injury. The following provide joint stability: the shape of the component, ligaments as they guide joints through the range of motion, vacuum created in the joint, and extensibility of the muscles and tendons.

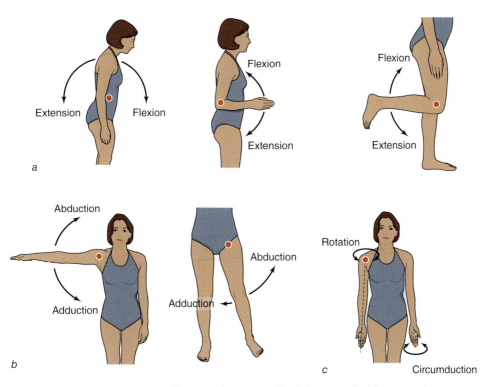

Figure 3.6 Joint movements: *(a)* flexion and extension; *(b)* abduction and adduction; and *(c)* rotation and circumduction.

Much of what is known about preventing dance injuries has been learned through the expertise of dance scientists, physical therapists, physicians, orthopedic surgeons, and sport trainers. It is important to listen to the advice of these professionals in preventing, diagnosing, and treating dance injuries. While your fellow dancers or even the dance teacher may have a lot of personal experience with injury, remember that they are not medical professionals, and any concerns about your health or healing should always involve the consultation of a health professional. Make sure the professional you consult is familiar with the unique needs of dancers.

PREVENTING AND TREATING COMMON DANCE INJURIES

Each person comes to dance class with a unique anatomy. No two bodies are exactly alike, and no two dancers respond to the physical demands of a dance class in the same way. This means that you will need to be very aware of how your body is feeling each time you begin a dance class. Don't assume the teacher can tell you have discomfort—let him know! Likewise, you should report new injuries to the instructor right away. Let him help you decide whether you should try to continue dancing, observe class that day, or seek medical attention. Never suffer silently through pain in dance class or rehearsal. Seek the advice of your teacher at the very least. Each school will have its own policy regarding whether a sick or injured dancer should observe class or stay home. A good rule is that if you are contagious, or potentially contagious, you

should stay home. If you are not feeling well enough to dance or are injured, you should come to class and observe and take notes. Taking notes on your observations is an excellent way to learn from a class without physically participating. You may gain valuable insights into ways to perform a particular skill that you have been working on by watching others in a way that is not possible when you are dancing. You also have the opportunity to observe the teacher's instructions and the students' responses. In this way your understanding can grow while your injury heals. There is no substitute for experience in dance, but it is far better to watch when you are ill or seriously injured for one class than to risk nonparticipation for a longer time by further injuring yourself or worsening your illness.

Most injuries occur as the result of improper muscle use, overuse of a particular muscle, or imbalance in muscle tone. In other words, if you develop a habit of poor joint alignment, you are more likely to get injured in a dance class rather than if you simply make a mistake as you are learning. Similarly, if you repeat the same exercises using the same muscles every time, you will overdevelop those muscles. Since muscles work in concert with each other, this can lead to an imbalance in muscle tone, and the complementary muscles to your strong ones become weak. This can also lead to injury. Sometimes injury occurs because the body is not sufficiently prepared. Sometimes dancers are overtired or undernourished and not paying careful attention to correct muscle use or skeletal alignment. If the wrong muscles are constantly used to perform a particular movement, then the correct muscles will eventually become underactive. This is a term physical therapists use to describe the weakness that results from underusing the proper muscles for an activity. When this cycle is repeated many times, it can lead to fatigue and injury.

Research indicates that the most common injuries in dancers are to the ankle, knee, and hip. These are often the result of muscle imbalance. Dancers tend to overstretch the hamstrings, adductors, and shin muscles while leaving the calves, quadriceps, and hip flexors tight. These imbalances cause fatigue and overuse injuries in many dancers. Proper stretching is one key to preventing injury.

Many of the factors in preventing dance injuries are provided for you by common sense and the structure of a dance class. Well-taught technique classes always provide a period of warming up, a period of intense physical activity, and a period of cooling down. This is exactly the pattern that fitness experts recommend for safe exercise. This also makes it essential for you to be on time for class. Tardiness may cause you to miss warm-up time that is necessary for safe participation.

Ask Questions

Asking the instructor when you have questions about what muscles to use or how your body should be aligned is also an important way to prevent injury. It ensures good form as you repeat exercises. It may seem to you that everyone knows the answer to your question, so you are reluctant to ask, but it is often the case that when one student asks a question, several others agree that they were equally unsure and the clarification helped them too. The teacher needs feedback and interaction so that he can teach a safe class. Good teachers value your questions, especially about proper form or alignment.

Ensure Proper Alignment

Nineteenth-century French exercise expert François Delsarte once said that grace is efficiency of motion. Efficient, correctly aligned use of the body prevents injury and enhances dance performance. Remember that the body is a closed system. This means if you are underusing one muscle, you are overusing another. The only way to correct this is to learn and be diligent about maintaining proper alignment. This means you will need to understand how the bones and muscles should

> **ACTIVITY** ▶▶▶▶▶▶▶▶▶▶▶▶▶
>
> ### Assessing Your Alignment
>
> Developing good alignment leads to efficient movement and is a habit of healthy living. To help you establish and maintain good alignment, think about alignment and do self-checks as you go through your daily routine. Check how you stand or walk at various times of the day and in various situations. Just doing three to five checks a day alerts you to your alignment and reminds you to think about alignment as you walk or stand.

be arranged for safe, clear movement. Information about basic alignment of the body is provided in more detail later in this chapter.

Recognize Illness and Fatigue

Use your common sense when it comes to dancing with illness or fatigue. Exercise physiologists do not recommend exercising with a fever because your body is not prepared to handle the demands of exercise when you are fighting an infection or already have a raised core body temperature. Many dancers attend class or rehearsal while ill because they are afraid to miss, but they end up infecting other dancers as a result because of the close physical contact during dance. Remember that if you are not feeling well, you can always observe class and take notes.

Manage Soreness

Some soreness is to be expected in the course of studying dance. This is not necessarily a symptom of injury; it is more likely a symptom of overuse of a muscle that hasn't had much attention recently. It can also indicate that you are pushing your body to new limits. The easiest cure for mild to moderate muscle soreness is to gently exercise the sore muscle. Do slow repetitions of a motion that uses the affected muscle or even a gentler version of the dance move that made you sore. Heat, massage, or a variety of ointments may relieve your pain temporarily, but they do not actually heal the sore muscle because they only reach the surface of the muscle. To really cure muscle soreness, you must increase the blood flow to the injured muscle with increased internal temperature. External treatments, as good as they feel to relieve pain, will only be temporary. Stretching increases blood flow and facilitates normal recruitment and relaxation patterns in muscles. This means you should allow additional time for gentle stretching during periods of soreness because the sore muscle will be tighter than normal and may feel stiff.

If your soreness does not go away with gentle repetitions, or within a reasonable time, such as 24 to 48 hours, you may be dealing with a dance injury. In general, you must do two things for any dance injury, whether it is a nagging pain that will not go away or a sudden severe pain that occurs: Evaluate and then treat. You will notice that ignoring it is not one of the options! Many dancers do not seek treatment at the beginning of an injury in the hopes that it will resolve itself. While this could be true in some instances, you will need to have a medical professional help you to make that determination. Similarly, rushing to treatment without careful evaluation of an injury can prolong your healing.

Use the PRICED Method

You can begin your treatment with the following simple guidelines, which is a method you can easily remember with the acronym **PRICED.** These letters stand for protect, rest, ice, compression, elevation, and diagnosis.

- **Protect.** Don't try to tough it out! This will likely only cause further damage to your tissues.
- **Rest.** Stop dancing so the injury can heal. While you are resting, observe what exactly you were doing when the pain occurred. What kind of pain is it—a dull ache or a stabbing pain? Where is its precise location? Did it happen on the first repetition or on the 10th?
- **Ice.** Applying ice to an injury cannot hurt you and should always be your first line of defense. Ice reduces swelling, which can begin to alleviate pain right away. Many dancers wonder whether to ice or heat an injury. Current advice from physical therapists is always to ice first. Elevate the injured body part above the heart, if possible, and then ice for no less than 20 minutes. Repeat this at least once an hour for the first 24 hours of an injury. Be sure to put two or three layers of fabric or a towel between you and the ice to prevent skin burns from the ice. The skin may naturally get pink as a result of icing. This should not concern you. If you do get a hive or extremely red skin under the ice, then you should remove it, since this is a more severe reaction, which could lead to a burn.
- **Compression.** To help reduce swelling, constrict the injured area by wrapping it with an elastic bandage. Compression does not mean you should wrap it

as tightly as possible. If you feel throbbing, unwrap the bandage and wrap it again more loosely. You should do the compression step only if you have an acute injury with swelling. Slowly developing dance injuries with no apparent swelling do not need this treatment.

- **Elevation.** Raise the injured area above the heart to help reduce swelling. Again, this is necessary only for an acute injury with swelling.

- **Diagnosis.** After 24 to 48 hours with an injury, be sure that you have seen a medical professional (a doctor, physical therapist, or athletic trainer).

Once you receive a clear diagnosis, the next phase of your treatment can begin. This will involve looking at your alignment and body mechanics to ensure safe practices and developing a recovery plan. This is where a physical therapist with knowledge of dance mechanics is important in your recovery because that professional can evaluate your alignment and then integrate correct alignment and training in body mechanics in your rehabilitation. Keep your dance teacher informed of the recovery plan so that he can help you in integrating back into dance class activities as they become appropriate for you.

Evaluate Recovery

In this critical phase of recovery from injury, you should reflect on how the injury occurred. Did it occur all of a sudden, or has this been building up for a while? Did you have a slight twisted ankle a week ago, which you didn't really rest, and now you have a more serious pain in your knee on the same leg? Are you working on a new piece of choreography or class exercise that demands repeated use of one part of your body? Are you sure you are executing this properly? Can you identify the muscle or joint that is causing you pain? Are certain motions of this joint more painful than others? The answers to all of these questions will help a medical professional determine the best course of treatment for you. If this is an **acute injury**, or one that occurs suddenly during the performance of a dance movement, or one that is so severe it prevents you from continuing, then you should consult a physician. While it is imperative to alert your teacher, director, or choreographer that you have been injured, remember that she is not a medical professional and that it is your responsibility to seek qualified help. Acute injury can also respond well to physical therapy. An acute injury, if not rehabilitated properly, can turn into a chronic injury. Proper flexibility, strength, endurance, and proprioception (the ability of the body to sense the position, location, orientation, and movement of its parts) needs to be restored after an injury to ensure your longevity as a dancer.

If you have an injury that has been building up over time, or a part of your body that frequently hurts you while dancing, then you have a **chronic injury**. It is equally important for the longevity of your dance life to deal with chronic injuries. For chronic injuries, an evaluation by a physician should be followed by consultation with a physical therapist. Physical therapists, especially those familiar with the needs of dancers, can give excellent long-term plans for treatment and recovery and can help you in facilitating those plans. This often involves exercise programs to help you strengthen weak muscles or connective tissue that is causing your chronic pain. Most college and university dance programs have a physical therapist you can consult, and many states allow treatment by a physical therapist without a prescription from a physician. Check with the director of your dance program or your teacher to see what services are available to you.

FLEXIBILITY AND STRETCHING

Muscles must be both strong and flexible to execute dance technique. In fact, muscle strength and flexibility will help with your overall ability to keep your body safe from injury. You need to learn not only what muscles are involved in doing a particular move but also how to strengthen and stretch them.

In addition to increasing flexibility, stretching provides several benefits:

- Reducing the risk of strain by reducing muscle tension
- Reducing the soreness of muscles
- Increasing mental and physical relaxation
- Promoting body awareness by learning to isolate muscle groups

It is valuable to stretch after warming up for class and after dance class, even if you are naturally flexible or if heightened flexibility is not your goal. You deserve the benefits of stretching—don't deprive yourself of this healthful practice!

Following are important safety and commonsense guidelines:

- **Be warm.** Stretches are much safer and more effective if your body is warmed up. Stretching should be the final phase of your warm-up routine, not the beginning of it.

Stretching is an important tool for developing as a dancer.

• **Stretching should not be painful.** Stretching may involve pushing yourself to make progress, but the process itself should not be painful. You should stretch to the point of tension in the muscle, not pain. If it is painful, back off of the stretch and take a look at your form. Seek expert eyes, if necessary, to help you understand where the pain is coming from, but do not accept pain as part of the process.

• **Don't bounce.** In general, proper stretches, even rhythmic ones, do not involve bouncing into a deeper stretch. Unfortunately, this was a popular method many years ago that has been handed down from many teachers to many students who then became teachers. Experts in modern kinesiology agree that this is not a safe practice.

• **Stretch for 30 to 60 seconds.** Dancers love to sit in stretches for several minutes at a time in the hopes that more time will mean more flexibility. This, too, has been proven untrue by modern science. Maximum benefit can be achieved in 30 to 60 seconds for each stretch if it is done in proper form. On the other side of this issue are people such as amateur runners who hold a calf stretch for 5 to 10 seconds before heading out on a run. This is not effective stretching, either. A minimum time for benefit applies as much as a maximum time.

• **You don't need to stretch every muscle every day.** If stretching is a regular part of your routine, you can easily change which muscle groups you stretch each day. This way the time for stretching fits more naturally into your schedule and doesn't become one more obligation that you will dread having to fulfill. Done properly, stretching is a relaxing, pleasant part of your life as a dancer. If you are having trouble deciding which muscle to stretch that day, just ask yourself which area you are worried about being sore. That is likely to be the muscle group or joint that most needs your attention. If you have used a muscle a lot, stretch it!

• **Stretch both sides evenly.** Don't forget to focus on each side equally. Dancers tend to focus on the muscles or leg that is more easily stretched. Doing this causes an imbalance in flexibility and can lead to injury. Stretch the right and left sides equally as long and with the same repetitions. If you notice an imbalance in one side over the other (for example, you notice your right hamstring is much more flexible than the left), then perform three more repetitions on the left side compared to the right until you feel you are getting a balance of flexibility in the muscle. Listen to your body, and don't always favor the good side! Symmetry in muscles is a key to reducing risk of injury, and this has been demonstrated in dance research.

• **Don't overstretch.** Stretching should focus on the muscles, since they have more elasticity than the tendons and ligaments. Connective tissue does not need to be overly elastic because its job is to hold the bones in the joint in place and to keep the muscles attached to the bones. Often dancers overstretch their connective tissue in the quest for more flexibility, but doing this can weaken the integrity of the joint and leave you prone to injury.

• **The danger of a stretch is relative to the person performing it.** There are not so much dangerous stretches as there are stretches that are dangerous for your particular body or state of fitness. The stretches that a yogi can do with years of training are not unsafe for her, but they may be quite unsafe for a beginning dancer. There are not unsafe stretches so much as unsafe stretching practices. The best guide to safety is to go slowly and to be patient and consistent with your body.

◆ **Don't keep the same routine with an injured muscle.** You should never stretch a strained muscle. If you have sharp pain while stretching, have recently fractured a bone, or the stability of the joint is in question, do not stretch that muscle. These are, of course, general recommendations. If you have any questions about how to treat an injured joint or muscle, seek advice from a qualified medical professional.

ACHIEVING OPTIMAL FITNESS

The body is your artistic instrument, and you need to keep it in good condition. Although dance classes can be considered a form of exercise, it is not sufficient exercise for achieving maximum physical fitness. Serious dancers should supplement their dance regimens with a program of physical fitness. There are five components of fitness:

1. **Body composition** is the proportion of fat and muscle in the body. It is a more accurate picture of fitness than weight alone. A thin person can still have a high body fat composition and be less healthy than a heavier person.
2. **Cardiorespiratory endurance** is the measure of stamina and efficiency of the heart and lungs.
3. **Muscular endurance** is the length of time that you can call on a particular muscle or muscle group to perform.
4. **Muscular strength** is the capacity of muscles to perform.
5. **Flexibility** is the range of motion of joints both at rest and during the performance of a physical activity.

To work on all of these elements, your exercise regimen should include aerobic training and muscle-strengthening activities. General recommendations are 2.5 hours of moderate-intensity aerobic work per week and 2 or more days of muscle-strengthening activities. Your muscle strengthening should be aimed at the legs, hips, abdomen, chest, shoulders, and arms. Dancers who pay a lot of attention to flexibility and muscular endurance but do not address body composition, cardiorespiratory endurance, and muscular strength may not really be as physically fit as they appear to be.

Many benefits to being physically fit are especially pertinent to dancers. In addition to the obvious advantages such as weight management and overall good health, exercise decreases blood pressure, raises levels of high-density lipoprotein (HDL, or "good" cholesterol), trains the body to handle physical and emotional stress, thins the blood so that the heart is more efficient and thereby lowers the risk of cardiovascular disease, and increases stamina. Fortunately, these benefits are systemic (that is, the entire body benefits, not just the legs, for example, when you are running). This is a remarkable tool for keeping your artistic instrument safe, healthy, efficient, and pain free. The time spent in effective exercise is a lifelong investment that will pay off in the studio, on the stage, and in daily activities.

What Dance Can and Cannot Do

Dancers would like to believe that the exercise gained from taking dance class is enough to make them physically fit. Unfortunately, this is only a myth. Although dance can be physically and mentally exhausting, it doesn't actually burn many calories. Dance scientists have determined that the average one-hour technique class burns only about 200 calories for women and 300 calories for men. A 30-minute well-structured aerobic workout can burn 250 calories for women, so dance is not even half as efficient (Chemlar & Fitt, 1990). Additionally, dance class consists of several intervals of high-intensity exercise alternated with periods of rest (the time when exercises are explained or you wait your turn to move across the floor). High-intensity interval training has been shown to use glucose, or sugar, as its primary fuel. This means that when you are in dance class, you are burning off the sugar in your bloodstream but not tapping into the body's fat reserves. To burn fat, low-intensity exercise for 30 minutes nonstop must occur (Bailey 1994).

In terms of muscle strength, there is good news and bad news for dancers. On the one hand, the high repetition of exercises in dance class will tone muscles well. In general, to tone a muscle, you exercise it with light weight (or no weight) and high repetition. To build muscular strength, you must lift heavier weight for fewer repetitions. So the good news is that dance leads to toned muscles. The bad news is that it doesn't necessarily lead to muscular strength. That is something that you should work on outside of the studio.

Making the Most of the Gym

Fortunately, there are many easy ways to improve your fitness and enhance your dancing outside of the dance studio. Most colleges and universities have fitness facilities that are readily available to students. The key is to make sure you are using the gym to your advantage. It is not unusual to see dancers who spend hours at the gym working intensely on cardio equipment but do not see the benefits of their time spent exercising because they are doing it so ineffectively or superstitiously. Exercise science, physical therapy, and dance science have a lot to teach dancers about taking advantage of the resources of a gym. Following are some basic recommendations, although every dancer could benefit from personal consultation with a physical therapist or qualified personal trainer, especially if these exercise recommendations do not seem to bring you to your goal.

An effective workout should begin with a 5- to 10-minute warm-up to increase heart rate and promote muscle elasticity and joint lubrication. This is followed by either an aerobic or strength training activity for 30 to 40 minutes and then a 5- to 10-minute cool-down. The cool-down should consist of a gradual slowing of the activity and then stretching once your heart rate has lowered. A slow cool-down will rid your muscles of lactic acid, a by-product of exercise that can cause soreness.

A balanced workout regimen will include days of strength training, days of cardiorespiratory training, and days of rest. The frequency of your workout will depend on how intense it is. The more intense the exercise, the more recovery time you will need. A more detailed explanation of how your body uses its primary fuels of sugar and fat appears in the nutrition section of this chapter, but for now, remember that your body burns calories and your muscles get stronger in the rest periods after exercise. In fact, you may burn as many calories *after* the workout as during the workout! Most exercise specialists recommend three days a week of aerobic work to maintain fitness and five days a week to improve fitness.

NUTRITION, HYDRATION, AND REST

Proper training improves dance; the same is true for nutrition. Proper nutrition can improve physical performance for both short-term and long-term health. To understand how proper nutrition improves dance performance, you must first understand the basics of exercise physiology and nutrition. Finally, rest is an essential component of dance training and recovery.

Nutrition

Like an automobile, your body requires fuel to move. Movement activity begins with the chemical bonds of food. These chemical bonds are called **macronutrients**, which consist of carbohydrate, protein, and fat. Although protein is important for tissue repair and regulatory purposes, the primary suppliers of energy are carbohydrate and fat. Carbohydrate is digested in the small intestine, absorbed, and then transported to the liver and muscles where it is stored as glycogen. The liver releases glycogen as glucose into the bloodstream to maintain normal blood-glucose levels. Glucose is used by the brain and skeletal muscles and can function as an immediate energy source. Because carbohydrate is the primary fuel you use during physical activity, it is critical that you consume carbohydrate on a daily basis. Trained athletes and dancers should consume 5 to 10 grams of carbohydrate per kilogram of body weight (Dunford 2006).

Proteins are complex organic compounds. The basic structures of protein are a chain of amino acids. They are important for tissue repair and regulatory purposes. Protein-containing foods are grouped as either complete or incomplete. Complete proteins such as those found in animal products (fish, eggs, milk) and some nonanimal products (such as quinoa) contain all nine essential amino acids. Incomplete proteins such as those found in most beans, nuts, and grains lack one or more of these essential amino acids and can be consumed in combination to form a complete protein. Vegans and vegetarians can consume a combination of beans, nuts, and grains to achieve their daily protein requirements. The protein requirement among dancers is the same as for any adult according to the current dietary reference intake (DRI), which is 0.8 gram per kilogram per day (Dunford 2006). Although many endurance- and resistance-trained athletes may need more protein, dancers usually are not considered endurance- or resistance-trained athletes.

Many dancers fear the word *fat*. However, fat is essential; it remains a major energy source, maintains body temperature, protects body organs, contributes to the satiety value of foods, and aids in the delivery and absorption of fat-soluble vitamins. Dietary fat is digested into fatty acids, absorbed in the small intestine, and stored as triglycerides in adipose tissue. These fatty acids can be used immediately for energy.

When to Eat

In addition to paying attention to what you should consume, you should pay attention to when you consume calories. Dancing without eating is an unsafe practice, since your muscles demand glucose for energy. If this doesn't come from your ingested food, then the body will get it from the muscles themselves. This means you will be weakening your muscles, just as you are putting a demand on them, leaving yourself open to injury. One hour before exercise, you should consume water and some carbohydrate and protein. Eat small amounts of food every three to four hours to help you avoid low blood sugar. Going more than five waking hours without food will cause your body to crave carbohydrate and usually results in overconsumption.

Vitamins and Supplements

Many dancers take daily vitamin and mineral supplements. Although this is a perfectly safe practice, you should remember that supplements are not the remedy for a poor diet. There is also no evidence that vitamins supply additional energy. In fact, there has not been a substance found that improves athletic performance that does not have the risk of substantial side effects. Vitamins can be overdosed with toxic results, so be sure not to exceed the recommended allowances for these. Herbal supplements, especially weight-loss supplements, are often nothing more than natural laxatives, so do not assume *herbal* is synonymous with *healthy*. Your best approach to good health and good energy is to improve the quality of your nutritional intake.

Hydration

What and when you drink are as important as what and when you eat. As you exercise or dance, you begin to sweat, which is water evaporating from your skin to cool the blood near the surface. This means there is less fluid in the blood, which can cause it to become thicker, which in turn means that needed oxygen is transported more slowly to your muscles. If the water is not replenished, then dizziness and dehydration can follow. Here are some simple guidelines for what and when you should drink:

- Drink a cup (8 oz., or ~240 ml) of water half an hour before you exercise or take dance class.
- Drink 3 to 6 ounces (~90-180 ml) of water every 15 to 20 minutes during dance class or rehearsal and during exercise if it lasts more than 20 minutes.

DID YOU KNOW? ▶▶▶▶▶▶▶▶▶

Rethink your drink: Coffee drinks, soda, alcohol, and sugary beverages may be tempting, but they offer little or no nutrition and can even lead to dehydration. Replacing one or more of these drinks with water during the day will rehydrate you and reduce the number of empty calories you consume.

- Drink cool fluids, around 40 to 50 degrees Fahrenheit (4-10 degrees Celsius). These are absorbed more quickly than warm or cold beverages.
- Drink 8 ounces of fluid 30 minutes after you dance or exercise.
- Before and during extended periods of dancing, drink only water.

Water is the best beverage to consume most of the time. After dancing for a long period, though, fruit juice may better nourish you. But during exercise or dance, the sugar in fruit juice is unnecessary, unless you are engaged in a long-term endurance sport.

Drink water as your body demands it. Nutritionists recommend that your caffeine intake not exceed 250 milligrams a day, the equivalent of two five-ounce cups of regular coffee. There is increasing research that indicates the artificial sweeteners in diet drinks cause hunger to increase and can actually lead to weight gain.

Rest

To prepare for dance class, you should be well rested. Along with proper nutrition and hydration, adequate rest supports recovery and revitalization. When muscles are overloaded, they need rest in order to rebuild themselves. Your mind also needs rest for optimal function. When you don't get enough rest, you become less alert and more prone to accidents. If you have trouble sleeping or are too anxious to rest, learn some relaxation techniques and pace yourself during your day so that your body and mind have time to rest.

SUMMARY

One of the great benefits of studying modern dance is that you learn more about how your body functions. By paying attention to the areas addressed in this chapter, you will better understand the amazing coordination of your muscles and skeleton when you dance. You have learned how to warm up and maintain your body, and you now know about the most common causes of injury for dancers. If you follow the advice in this chapter regarding physical fitness and warming up, you will have a successful and enjoyable experience in modern dance and the keys to longevity as a dancer. By following the nutrition and hydration guidelines in this chapter, you will be able to fuel your body to achieve peak performance. Learning and understanding how your body works physically is not only valuable for a fulfilling modern dance experience but vital for a satisfying life experience, too!

To find supplementary materials for this chapter, such as learning activities, e-journal assignments, and web links, visit the web resource at **www.HumanKinetics.com/BeginningModernDance1E.**

WEB RESOURCE

Basics of Modern Dance

One of the most stimulating and challenging parts of a modern dance class is learning new movements and ways to put movements together. Some of these movements overlap with other genres of dance, and some are unique to modern dance. Once you learn the building blocks of the art form, you will feel more comfortable participating and expressing yourself in this medium.

This chapter introduces some of the basic ideas in modern dance. An overall view of the concepts and movement principles used in this genre of dance can prepare you to absorb the concepts covered in modern dance class more readily. A deeper understanding of the art form will help you to make movement, not just imitate it. Familiarity with the basic styles of modern dance can also make your movement experiences more satisfying because you will see how what you are doing in the studio connects to a 100-year-old tradition of physical and artistic expression. This chapter looks at concepts, movement principles, and basic positions and movements of the body.

ELEMENTS OF DANCE

Many of the concepts of the body's movement in space in modern dance rely on the teachings of the 19th- and early 20th-century Hungarian movement theorist and educator **Rudolf von Laban**. Laban devised an intricate analytical method for describing the myriad of movement possibilities for the human body. His system, referred to as **Laban movement analysis,** or LMA, continues to be studied today around the world. The principles of this system offer a large vocabulary for describing where in space the body is moving and the quality of the movements themselves. This system of analyzing movement has been the foundation for many fields. It is used by rehearsal directors, actors, choreographers, and dance/movement therapists to provide a common vocabulary for understanding the way humans move in both performance contexts and in everyday life.

Laban's early students were some of the most influential pioneers of modern dance, such as Mary Wigman, often seen as the mother of modern dance in Germany. Laban's work developed at the same time as modern dance was born in the beginning of the 20th century, and many of his principles of movement were a natural incorporation into the art form. While it is beyond the scope of this text to go into great detail on all the principles of LMA, there are several fundamental ideas from Laban's work that will help you to understand the basic movements and aesthetics of modern dance.

The four essential ways in which Laban divided his analysis of movements was in the areas of body, space, shape, and effort. Body refers to all the anatomical ways in which the body moves based on developmental progression, including initiation, sequencing, breath, support, and phrasing. **Space** concerns pathways, levels (meaning close or far from the floor), and clarity in the directions the body can move. Shape denotes how the body contours transform and adapt as it moves through space. What is most important to know for the purposes of looking at the basics of modern dance, however, is the fourth element, what Laban called the four efforts (Newlove & Dalby, 2004). These are terms that you will hear quite frequently in modern dance classes. These elements are space, time, weight, and flow. Let's consider each of these in turn.

Space

This element refers to the way in which you relate to space. You could be approaching the space in a linear fashion, going directly from one place to another, or you could be aware of all of the space around you. From this perspective, the body's use of space is either direct or indirect.

Direct movements have clear definable paths in space. When you want to draw someone's attention to something, you use your finger to point directly to it. The path that your finger takes in that simple gesture is direct. The opposite of this is **indirect movement.** These are movements that have a multidirectional or more roundabout path through space. When you are wandering through a carnival or fair, your path from attraction to attraction is indirect.

Time

In musical terms, **time** refers to rhythm or the use of a beat or pulse. In dance, however, time does not need music or a steady beat in order to exist. Time in dance relates more to the duration of a movement. Specifically, time in Laban effort terms relates to your attitude about time—whether it seems to move slow or fast. Laban described movement as either **quick** or **sustained.** Just as they sound, quick movements are of a short duration, and sustained movements are of a longer duration. When you put your hand on a hot stove by accident, the movement to remove it is a quick one. When you pet the especially luxurious coat of a long-haired cat, your hand moves in a slow, sustained way.

Weight

The quality of **weight** affects the look and feel of movement as well. In terms of Laban principles, weight is the pull of gravity on the body. Some movements resist gravity, and some movements indulge in it. Laban referred to this continuum of weighted qualities as movements being between **strong** and **light**. A strong movement is one in which there is a lot of firmness and power or indulgence in gravity. A light movement is one in which there is less apparent effect of gravity. Raise your arm and then lower it as if it is made of a very heavy metal. This is strong weight. Raise your arm again and now lower it as if it consists of feathers. This is a light quality of weight.

Flow

The fourth element is **flow**, which describes how continuous a movement is. This dimension is measured by the continuum of free and bound. **Free flow** is movement that is connected and continuous; think of water flowing downstream or hair in the wind. **Bound flow** is the opposite end of the continuum. This is movement that is tight, contained, careful, and discontinuous. It has a starting-and-stopping quality to it. Think of riding in a car over cobblestone roads.

The elements of space, time, weight, and flow can be used to describe any movement. None of them is inherently good or bad in modern dance. Jerky movements have their place in choreography just as smooth ones do. Sometimes a strong movement is called for, sometimes a light one, and so on. It may help you to pick up movement combinations or exercises faster if you begin to recognize these qualities in the movement. Certainly when it comes time to audition for performances, understanding not only the specific steps that you are being asked to do, but the qualities with which you are expected to do them, could be exactly the competitive edge you need to be cast in a piece. No matter what kind of movements you are asked to do in dance, the efforts (space, time, weight, and flow) are the building blocks for understanding the movements themselves.

Approach to the Kinesphere

In addition to looking at the way that space is traversed, Laban gives directional guidelines to describing space. These guidelines orient the body within a sphere of movement called the **kinesphere**. This is the amount of space around your body that extends to the ends of where you can reach in each direction. Where you are within the space of the kinesphere—whether you are reaching behind yourself or in front of yourself—can be described as happening in three intersecting planes of movement, or planes of space.

Dimensional Planes

The three planes of space that Laban describes to quantify the understanding of where the body is moving are called the **dimensional planes**. These three planes intersect at the center of the body. Imagine yourself as the center of your own kinesphere. Now stretch your arms above your head directly up from the shoulders, and open your legs as wide as they can comfortably go. You are now demonstrating the **vertical plane,** also known as door plane. This is the plane that describes how high and low the movement dimension may be. Next, imagine that you are at the exact center of a table, like the umbrella in the middle of an outdoor patio table. Open your arms around you at waist height and you will experience the **horizontal plane**, or table plane. This is the dimension that describes reaching from side to side all around you. Finally, extend your right hand directly in front of you and your left hand directly behind you. Plant your feet so that your right foot is also forward and your left foot is back. You are now standing in the **sagittal plane**, or wheel plane. This dimension is the one that includes the distance you can reach forward and backward in your kinesphere. Figure 4.1 shows the dimensional cross of the three planes as Laban conceived of it.

Thinking of the space around you in this way offers some landmarks for positions of the body. Imagine reaching to the top of the vertical plane. This is the high direction all around you. If you were to reach to the front of you in the high direction, this is referred to as forward high. If you reach to the back and in the low level, this becomes back low. This specific information can help you to understand exactly where your arms, legs, hips, and torso will be oriented in any given shape.

Levels

Another way of looking at yourself in space is to use the floor beneath you as a landmark. This is called the use of **level** in dance. Laban saw people as moving in one of three

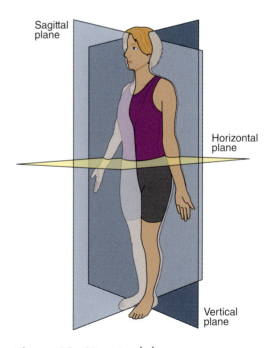

Figure 4.1   Dimensional planes.

spaces with respect to the floor. You could move high, or as far away from the floor as possible, which would include reaching, jumping, and leaping. You could also move on the low level, which includes earthbound movements, such as deep bending or rolling. And you could move in the middle level, which is between the extremes of high and low, or in the center space of your kinesphere. The dynamic use of levels is an important tool of modern dance choreographers in creating variety in dance.

MOVEMENT PREFERENCES IN MODERN DANCE

Now that you have a grasp of the way in which modern dance looks at movement, the next step is to understand how these movement efforts of space, time, weight, and flow are frequently used in modern dance. Each genre of dance uses the same instrument, the human body. How, then, is modern dance different from other types of dance? The answer to this question lies in the ways in which movements are put together and also in the aesthetic preferences of the art form. In this section you will learn about these preferences in modern dance that are true for all styles of the form. These preferences include centrally initiated movement, breath, integrated body, preference for flow over shape, and countertension.

These preferences in ways of moving are equal in importance in modern dance; one is not more central or more common than the others. If you listen to the directions that modern dance teachers give, and you pay close attention to the feedback or corrections that you and other dancers receive in class, you will likely hear these ideas mentioned frequently. Sometimes the application of one of these ways of moving is the difference between a well-executed movement and a passable one. Running through the space and holding your breath, for example, will not look or feel the same as running through the space using a deep exhalation. Let's look at each of these preferences individually.

Centrally Initiated Movement

Movements in modern dance frequently start from the middle of the body, using the muscles of the abdomen, often coupled with an exhalation. This is what is meant by centrally initiated movement; it begins in the center of the body. You may notice that your teacher begins class with exhaling and curving in the middle or even sitting on the floor and rounding the center of the torso. There are several reasons for this.

Modern dance began in an era when women wore corsets. They couldn't easily move their torsos or even breathe deeply in many cases. The early women who pioneered the field of modern dance removed their corsets and watched what happened as their breath moved through their upper bodies. You can try this yourself. Look in the mirror at your torso as you exaggerate your breathing, and you will see the beginnings of the movement called a **contraction**. This forward and backward curving of the torso is central to all forms of modern dance. Some styles contract higher in the torso and some lower, and some twist this movement to the side, but no matter how it is done, it is a central part of the vocabulary. The early modern dancers felt this movement showed a sense of freedom from the physical constraints of the corset but also from the political restrictions that it implied. The beginnings of modern dance are tied to the first wave of feminism, and the symbol of the torso moving without a corset was a way of showing the desire to shed the limitations placed on women at the time.

Another reason that so much modern dance movement begins in the center of the body may relate once again to Laban. The imaginary dimensional cross, from which Laban begins movement description, intersects at the center of the torso. It literally is the center of movement from this perspective. The early part of the 20th century, when modern dance began, was a time of scientific discovery. The popularity of a scientific, analytical way to look at movements may have been a powerful framework for the early modern dance pioneers. There is a strong possibility that Laban's way of framing movement influenced the pioneers' ways of creating modern dance.

Breath

The use of breath is one of the movement principles that unite all the various styles of modern dance. Breath is a central force of nature and a sustaining element of life. Many of the modern dance pioneers were interested in how the body in motion connected to the natural world. They wanted to know how the body was like the motion of the sea or the elements of the natural world, and this necessitated paying attention to the rhythms of the body through breathing. Perhaps because the early pioneers explored it so fully when they removed their corsets or when they were attempting to connect to nature, or perhaps because it is simply central to an athletic use of the body, breath is often discussed in modern dance class. Movements can come from exhaling or inhaling. Often you will be instructed to look at the pattern of your breathing as you move through a dance sequence. Do not be surprised if you are asked to make your breath audible with a loud exhalation! Paying attention to your breathing can make some sequences easier to execute but can also enhance your emotional and physical investment in the movements. As you tie your breathing to your actions, you are using more of yourself as you dance.

Integrated Body

All dance forms rely on moving the parts of the body in harmony. What that harmony looks like, however, varies from dance form to dance form. In modern dance, using the body as a whole is often a preference. It is impossible to make statements of absolutes in the arts. Some modern dance choreographers use isolation as part of their vocabulary, but in general, a fully integrated use of the body is a principle of modern dance. This means that as you execute even the smallest movement, your entire body is involved. As you reach upward, you involve your legs in rooting downward to the earth. When you push your arms forward, you allow your chest to respond. While dancing correctly in every form of dance requires you to pay attention to your whole body, especially where alignment is concerned, the movements of modern dance encourage you to integrate your arms, legs, spine, and torso together to create the movements of the dance form rather than isolating any one part of the body. Twentieth-century modern dance choreographer José Limón said that the body is like an orchestra. Each part of the body is one section of the group. While sometimes the violins (or let's say the arms and chest) are taking the lead, the entire orchestra is involved in the music. Keep this in mind when you are learning new movements. If you ask yourself how the whole body is responding to the instruction and which part of your body's "orchestra" is playing the loudest, you may find the movements easier and more fulfilling to execute.

Preference for Flow Over Shape

While shape is an important part of using the body to make art in modern dance, the form is not geared only to shape, line, and poses. In fact, the flow, or transition from one shape to another, is just as important in modern dance as the actual shapes themselves. In many movement combinations, shapes are used to travel through space, or one shape turns right into another. As you learn new movement sequences in modern dance class, ask yourself whether you are expected to make the shape of the body distinct or if the instructor intends for you to blend one shape into another. This quality of continuity can be a distinctive feature of the movements you are learning.

Countertension

One principle originally described by Laban that is frequently seen in modern dance is the concept of **countertension**, which means giving equal energy to two opposing parts of the body. If you extend your right leg behind you and your left arm in front of you and reach each in the directions they are pointing with equal energy, you are using countertension. It is a way for you to create an energetic connection, or tension, between these parts of the body. This way of approaching the movement not only strengthens the pose you are in but also gives the body a very different look than if you were only paying attention or giving energy to one of the two body parts. In some modern techniques, this countertension is used to heighten the feeling of diagonals that cross the body; in other kinds of modern dance, it is used to find a tension or energy between the dancers' upward motion while maintaining a strong connection to the floor.

Holding countertensions in the body doesn't mean that you need to always be exactly on balance. In

ACTIVITY ▶▶▶▶▶▶▶▶▶▶▶

Countertension

Often the opposition to your energy can come from another dancer, not only from another body part. Face another dancer and hold each other's hands so that your right hand is holding your partner's left and your left is holding your partner's right. Slowly pull away from each other with equal force without letting go. The energy that is created between you is a powerful force for partnering work in modern dance. This countertension can be between any two dancers as partners, regardless of sex.

fact, the idea of falling off balance is often considered beautiful in modern dance. This is the difference between **stabile** and **labile**. Stabile is where the body is balancing; labile is where the body is off of equilibrium. The excitement of nearly losing balance and then regaining it adds vitality and dynamics to the vocabulary of modern dance movement.

These preferences for ways of moving will be combined with the basic steps and positions of modern dance in your classes. You will need to learn the basic movement vocabulary of modern dance, made up of basic positions, locomotor and nonlocomotor movements, and these preferences in order to be a successful modern dancer.

BASIC POSITIONS

While there is certainly a difference between styles of modern dance in what steps, positions, and shapes are used, certain basic positions are shared among all of the various styles of dance that fit under the umbrella of modern dance. Some of these are borrowed from ballet and may carry these same terms over into modern dance class. These basic positions will be useful in understanding the codified techniques introduced in chapter 8 of this book.

Parallel Foot and Leg Positions

Modern dance uses many positions of the feet, including flexed and pointed. A **flexed foot** is one in which the toes are brought upward so that the ankle joint is flexed at a right angle in relation to the leg. In a **pointed foot,** the toes and top of the foot are extended to form one long line from the front of the shin through the toes. All forms of modern dance also use a position called **parallel**. This means that the legs are situated so that the knees and toes face forward.

Parallel First

The most common of the parallel positions is **parallel first**. Stand with your feet directly under your hips with your toes facing forward in front of you. This is parallel first (figure 4.2). Be sure when you bend your knees that they line up with the center of your foot and you are not allowing your knees to come together in this position. This will ensure good alignment of the legs for traveling and jumping.

Figure 4.2   Parallel first position.

Parallel Second

If you separate your feet somewhat wider than your hips but keep the feet and toes facing forward, you will be in a position most styles of modern dance call **parallel second** (figure 4.3).

Parallel Fourth

Now take your right foot in front of you so that the back of your heel is just past the toes on your left foot. This position is called **parallel fourth** (figure 4.4). This is the right side. Reverse your feet for parallel fourth on the left.

Turned-Out Foot and Leg Positions

In addition to positions in parallel, modern dance uses positions that stem from the ballet tradition. These positions are all with turned-out legs.

Turnout refers to the rotation of the hips and legs away from the midline of the body. Put your feet together with the heels and toes touching in parallel. Now from your hip joints, rotate your legs outward as far as they will comfortably go while keeping your heels together and toes apart. This is a **turned-out position**. Some people have a wide degree of natural turnout due to more flexible hip sockets. Do not overrotate your legs, which can cause injury. To check for overrotation, bend your knees slightly. The center of your knee should line up directly over the middle toes of your foot. If your knee is not lined up with the middle toes, adjust your turnout inward until you find the true line of your legs. For most beginning

Figure 4.3   Parallel second position.

Figure 4.4   Parallel fourth position.

dancers, this is approximately a 90-degree angle. This will widen with proper training, but it is important not to force it into position. With turned-out legs, there are five positions of the feet used in modern dance that have been borrowed from the traditions of ballet and retain their ballet names.

First Position

If you are standing with your heels together and your toes apart with your legs properly turned out from the hips, then you are standing in **first position**. In modern class, since parallel first is used just as frequently, you may hear this position referred to as **turned-out first** (figure 4.5).

Figure 4.5 Turned-out first position.

Second Position

If you take one foot and extend it to the side and then set it down while still turned out, just slightly wider than the hips, this is **second position**, or **turned-out second** (figure 4.6).

Figure 4.6 Turned-out second position.

Third Position

Now move your right foot inward so that the heel of your right foot is in the middle of the arch of your left. You are now in **third position**, or **turned-out third** (figure 4.7). This can be done on both sides.

Figure 4.7   Turned-out third position.

Fourth Position

From first position, extend your right foot in front of you and set the heel down so that the right heel and the left big toe are one of your feet's length apart. This is **fourth position**, or **turned-out fourth** (figure 4.8). This can be done on both sides. In many ballet classes and some modern classes, fourth position is not taken from first but from third position so that the legs are more crossed. This will be up to your instructor to decide how you should find fourth position.

Figure 4.8   Turned-out fourth position.

Fifth Position

Return to third position. Instead of putting your right heel at the midline of your left foot, put it at your left big toe. This is **fifth position**, or **turned-out fifth** (figure 4.9). As with third and fourth, this position can be done on both sides.

Arm Positions

Just as some common positions of the legs and feet have names, there are common positions of the arms that have specific names. There is a great deal of variety in terminology for the arms, however. This may be because different styles of ballet use different numbering systems for the arms. You will also find in modern dance class that specific terminology for traditional arm positions may not be used simply because there are many varieties of arm positions in modern dance, and many teachers do not use the traditionally balletic ones. In case your teacher does use this terminology, or in case you would like to experiment with variations of these in your own movement choices, let's review the most common positions of the arms.

First Position

In **first position of the arms,** both arms are down at your sides with a slight curve to the elbow as if there is a little air directly under the armpit. Your fingers are slightly separated and rest at the middle of your thighs (figure 4.10).

Figure 4.9   Turned-out fifth position.

Figure 4.10   First position of the arms.

Second Position

Second position of the arms refers to having both arms to the side of the body at about a 90-degree angle from your torso. In this position the arms are also a little curved, with the palms facing straight forward of the body, or tilted slightly downward (figure 4.11). Your teacher will clarify which variation she prefers, but in all variations, the shoulders should not be lifted but should be relaxed into position with the muscles of the upper back supporting the arms. Second position is probably the most common arm position that you will encounter in modern dance class.

Figure 4.11   Second position of the arms.

Third Position

Raise one arm so that it is curved directly overhead. This is **third position of the arms** (figure 4.12).

Figure 4.12   Third position of the arms.

Fourth Position

Raise the curved arm in front of you so that it is overhead, and you will have **fourth position of the arms** (figure 4.13). Third and fourth positions of the arms have many variations, and your teacher will clarify which position you should use in any particular exercise.

Figure 4.13 Fourth position of the arms.

Fifth Position

Raise both arms so that they are overhead with a slight curve to them. This is **fifth position of the arms** (figure 4.14).

Figure 4.14 Fifth position of the arms.

Floor Positions

Modern dancers believe that the earth, and subsequently the floor, is a source of strength. Because of this connection, a section of modern dance class takes place while seated or lying on the floor of the dance studio. A vocabulary of positions related to the use of the floor has developed from this practice.

The X

Some teachers begin the floor portion of the class by lying in

Figure 4.15   The X.

the **X**. Based on the work of physical therapist Irmgard Bartenieff, this shape is just what it sounds like. Stand in a wide second position with your hands above your head reaching high on both sides. Now repeat this position lying on your back on the floor (figure 4.15). You are now in the X. This is an excellent position for feeling the diagonal tensions in the body. Extend your left arm and right leg as you lie there. You do not need to be concerned about balance as you reach, so you are free to experiment with the energy flow between the parts of your body.

In addition to lying on the floor, you can do part of the floor work in modern dance class while seated. There are four basic positions of the legs in seated floor work.

Tailor Sit

Sitting with the soles of your feet together is usually termed the **tailor sit** position. You may have experienced this as a butterfly stretch in your physical education classes in school. The difference is that you do not want to pull your feet in as close to you as possible; rather, your feet should be at an appropriate distance away from your torso so that you can sit comfortably with your back straight and your shoulders positioned over your hips in good alignment (figure 4.16).

Figure 4.16   Tailor sit.

First Position on the Floor

First position on the floor involves sitting with both legs extended directly in front of you. You may have the knees facing upward, so your legs are in parallel, or have the knees facing more toward the sides so that you are in a turned-out first position on the floor (figure 4.17).

Figure 4.17 First position on the floor.

Second Position on the Floor

Second position on the floor, just like a standing second position, is an open position with the legs open as wide as they can go without rolling forward and with the back comfortably upright at a right angle to the legs (figure 4.18). As in first position on the floor, the legs can be parallel or turned out in this floor position. Many dancers are eager to have a wide separation in their legs in this position, so they force their legs wider than good alignment allows. To maintain alignment in this position, face the knees up to the ceiling or roll them outward to open the legs into a turned-out position.

Figure 4.18 Second position on the floor with *(a)* feet pointed and *(b)* feet flexed.

Fourth Position on the Floor

Fourth position on the floor (figure 4.19) is a seated position in which the front leg is bent in front of you with the knee to the outside of your body and the foot toward the midline of your body. Your back leg is also bent but at a right angle to the first leg with the foot pointing behind you. The toes of your front leg will likely touch the knee of your back leg. Again, if you cannot sit upright with good spinal alignment in this position, then you

Figure 4.19 Fourth position on the floor.

should separate the legs somewhat until your flexibility increases. Some instructors teach this position with both hips on the floor so that the front knee needs to come off the floor slightly. Other teachers insist that the front knee be on the floor, so many dancers will not have the opposing hip firmly on the floor. Depending on the style of modern dance and the specific exercise, the teacher will advise you on which to select if your body is not able to accommodate both the knee and the opposing hip on the floor at the same time. It is always appropriate to ask questions about this or any other issues of alignment, since your question may be one that many dancers have and everyone could benefit from clarification.

STAGE DIRECTIONS

Whatever the shape of the body in motion, it is also useful to articulate the orientation of the body in relation to the space in the room or on the stage. These orientations are called **stage directions** (see figure 4.20). The basic stage directions for dance are the same as they are for theater. The front of the stage is downstage, and the back of the stage is upstage. The sides of the stage are based on the perspective of the performer, so if you are standing on the stage facing an audience, stage right is to your right. If you are standing on the stage facing the audience, stage left is to your left. When the instructor tells the class to start the combination stage right, he means the right side of the dance studio when you are facing the mirror.

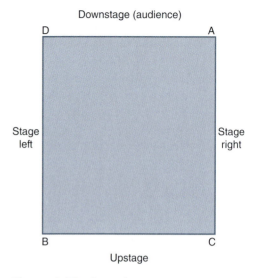

Figure 4.20 Stage directions.

BASIC MOVEMENTS

As with the basic positions, modern dance shares some basic movements with other genres of dance. Frequently these movements have their own names that are particular to the style of modern dance taught. Many basic movements, however, share the same terminology as their counterparts. More important is that you have a basic understanding of the movements to which these terms refer. Movements fall into two rough categories: **nonlocomotor,** or stationary, and **locomotor,** or traveling through space.

▶ Nonlocomotor Movements

Many of the nonlocomotor movements described in this chapter have their origin in classical ballet. Usually modern dance teachers have experience in ballet, so it is not unusual for these terms to be used in a modern dance technique class.

Plié

A **plié** is a bending of the knees. In can be done from any position but is frequently practiced in the five traditional positions of ballet, just covered.

Demi-Plié and Grande Plié

When your knees bend as deeply as possible while you keep your back straight and in good alignment, this is a **grande plié**. If the knees are bent only partially with the heels remaining on the floor, then this is a **demi-plié**. The one exception to this rule, however, is a second position grande plié. In this position, the heels remain on the floor. The demi-plié and grande plié in second position are differentiated by degree. The demi-plié and grande plié in second position are higher (demi-plié) or deeper (grande plié) versions of the same movement.

Battement Tendu

Often shortened to tendu, the **battement tendu** is one of the fundamental movements of the foot and leg. This action occurs when you extend your foot to a full point while keeping the knee straight and the foot in contact with the floor. You can extend the tendu in a number of directions, mostly straight in front of you, to the side of you, or behind you. In class exercises, tendus are often done in a sequence of front, side, back, side. This is referred to as moving **en croix**, or in the shape of a cross. In modern dance, en croix can be done in either parallel or turned-out positions of the legs.

The leg that is performing the tendu is referred to as the working leg. The leg on which you are standing is referred to as the standing leg. The leg itself performing the tendu can be in either parallel or turnout. Your teacher will specify which to use.

Dégagé

If you were to execute the tendu motion with a bit more energy and allow it to leave the floor just slightly, you would have a movement called a **dégagé**. The foot disengages from the floor to point, but the knee remains straight. Like the related tendu, this is often done en croix and can be done in either parallel or turnout.

Grand Battement

The basic movement that began as a tendu increased in size to a dégagé and can be increased further to become a grand battement, or simply a battement. This movement begins with the tendu extension of the foot and straight knee, but the leg is then lifted high off the floor, past the dégagé. A battement can extend to a 90-degree angle to the body or even higher, as long as the standing leg and alignment of the back are not affected. This movement is also commonly done en croix and can be done in parallel or turnout.

Passé

A common position is to raise one leg off the floor by bending that knee and placing the pointed foot of the leg you just bent near the knee of your other straight standing leg (figure 4.21). This position is called passé.

Figure 4.21   Passé position.

Développé

The **développé** is similar to a battement, except that rather than keeping the knee straight, you unfold it from the knee. Lift your leg into passé so that the pointed toe goes near your knee, then extend that leg forward or to the side or behind you. This movement can be done in parallel or turnout.

Relevé

The term **relevé**, or more accurately three-quarter relevé, refers to balancing on all five toes and the metatarsals (ball of the foot) with legs straight and heels lifted off the floor. You can do this balance in any position of the feet, on one foot while balancing, or while traveling or turning.

Forced Arch

A position and movement related to relevé that is unique to modern dance is **forced arch**. This is the combination of relevé and plié. Rise on your feet so that your heels are off the floor and you are balancing on the balls of your feet in relevé. Now keep the heels off the floor and bend your knees. Your feet and legs are now in a forced arch. While you can hold this as a position, it is also frequently used as a movement in transition from relevé to plié.

▶ Arclike and Successive Movements

Another consideration is the way in which arms or legs arrive at their positions. In modern dance, a limb has two basic pathways. Its movement is either arclike or successive.

Arclike means the limb moves as one piece from the shoulder joint (in the case of the arm) or from the hip (in the case of the leg). For example, if you move your arm from your side to above your head without bending at the elbow but by swinging it from the shoulder joint, this is an arclike, or radial, movement.

If you lower that same arm by bending the elbow and then the wrist, articulating each joint along the way, this is a **successive,** or spokelike, movement. Both are common ways to move your arms or legs, so pay close attention to not only the position of the limb but also its path to that position.

Arm Swing

In many styles of modern dance, the arms are used in a fluid, swinging manner. The arm can begin overhead and swing downward to the front or the back, or it can begin at the side of the body and swing across the body or overhead. No matter what the path of the arms, the arm swing should respond to gravity. Rather than place the arm down with complete control, in an **arm swing** you allow it to fall with weight. This will cause the arm to **rebound,** or carry some natural momentum with it.

Leg Swing

A **leg swing** occurs when the leg is lifted and allowed to fall in response to gravity and then rebound upward. The most common leg swing combinations involve swinging from the hip in the attitude, or bent knee, position. The leg can swing back to front, front to back, or side to side.

Body Swing

Like the arm and leg swings, a **body swing** responds to gravity. Most often beginning with the arms above the head, drop your upper body to curve over the legs and swing back up. This is frequently done with bent knees to enhance the natural rebound to return the upper body to a straight standing position. Body swings can be done from side to side as well. These are frequently combined with arm swings or leg swings.

Bending and Twisting

The torso is an expressive and active part of movement in modern dance. Many of the opening exercises in a modern dance class focus on learning various ways to bend your upper body. These include not only forward and back but side bends as well. Allow your head to follow through with the line of the bend so that the arc of your bend goes from the top of your head smoothly through to your hips. It is not uncommon for the upper body to bend in opposition to the position of the hips, which is known as a **twist.**

Tilt

When the body shifts to the side onto one leg without bending the torso, this is known as a **tilt**. The shoulders stay in alignment over the hips, and the entire shape of the body shifts to one side.

Rising and Falling

Many movements in modern dance require the body to rise off the floor and return back to lying or sitting. This is known as rising and falling. The reverse pattern is also frequently used, where you go from standing to sitting, rolling, or lying on the floor and then return to a standing position. There are nearly as many ways to rise and fall as there are modern dance teachers! The rising and falling movement is a common part of the modern dance vocabulary, so it is mentioned here as a basic nonlocomotor movement, but it is not one specific step that you will learn. This combination of movements is sometimes referred to as falling and recovering.

Contraction

A **contraction** is pulling inward and tensing the center of the body. Some styles of modern dance contract low in the torso close to the pelvis, some in the center of the torso near the stomach, and others somewhat higher, nearer the chest. When your teacher instructs you to contract, pay attention to where she is articulating the movement.

Release

A **release** is the countering movement to a contraction. It means to relax the tension from the contraction and return to a neutral position.

Arch

An **arch** is the opposite of a contraction, where the upper body curves backward rather than forward as it does in response to a contraction. The line of the arch should not pinch the neck and shoulders or cramp the neck; it should have one continuous line from the chest through to the top of the head.

▶ Locomotor Movements

Modern dance uses a variety of movements that travel through space. It would not be possible to list all of the ways that you can move through space as a dancer, but following are some of the most common traveling movements used in a modern dance class.

The seven **basic locomotor movements** are walk, run, hop, jump, slide, gallop, and skip. Although walking and running require no explanation, there are important distinctions between the other locomotor movements.

- A **hop** is a jump on one foot.
- A **jump** involves leaving the floor using both feet at the same time.
- A **slide** moves sideways through space with the feet alternating between being open and closed. Either foot can lead in a slide.
- A **gallop** also alternates between open and closed feet but moves forward in space. You can alternate the lead foot in a gallop as well.
- A **skip** is an alternating combination of a step and a hop.

In addition to the basic ways of moving, you will learn a number of more complex ways to travel through the space. Some of these will take a considerable amount of practice and may not be perfected as a beginner, but that is the joy of studying an art form! Modern dance can provide you with interesting movement challenges for a long time.

Prance

A **prance** is a stylized walk in which the feet are placed in front of the body rather than directly under the legs. This necessitates bringing the knees a little higher and forward than you would do in a normal walk. Prancing is usually done at a quicker tempo so that it approximates a hopping quality.

Leap

A **leap** is a jump in which you transfer your weight from one foot to the other. A leap can be long, short, high, or low. There are many variations in which the legs stay straight and others that have one or the other leg bent. The one common element among all leaps is going from one foot to the other as you travel through space.

Chassé

A **chassé** is a way of traveling across the floor by stepping with one foot, bringing the second foot to meet it, and then extending the original foot outward again. Your first step begins with a bent knee, and your feet should touch in the air in the middle of this step–together–step pattern.

Triplet

A **triplet** is a series of three steps, usually with the pattern of down–up–up. In the down step the knees are bent, and in the up step the knees are straight and the heel is raised.

Grapevine

The **grapevine** step, found in many folk dances, travels sideways by walking with a crossing pattern, where the feet alternate between stepping front and behind. A common form of the grapevine begins with stepping one foot over the other on count 1, stepping side on count 2 with the second foot, stepping behind with the first foot on count 3, and stepping side again on count 4 with the second foot. An open grapevine is one in which the pattern begins by stepping side instead of crossed.

▶ Turns

You will encounter many turns in a modern dance class. Some travel in space and others remain stationary. Your teacher will let you know which turn to use. The most common kinds of turns you are likely to encounter are the chaîne and the three-step turn.

Chaîne

A **chaîne turn** involves making a full revolution every two steps. You step on alternating feet each turn. It can be performed in succession so that you have several traveling turns in a row.

Three-Step Turn

A **three-step turn** begins with one foot extended. You step onto the ball of your extended foot, making a half turn. With the next step on the second foot, you complete the turn to the front. Step one more time on your first foot and bend your knee so that you have the second foot extended. You are now ready to repeat the turn to the other side.

Many basic positions and movements make up the vocabulary of modern dance. These are the building blocks of using the body as an expressive medium and the keys to participating fully in a modern dance class.

SUMMARY

The ideas that Rudolf von Laban articulated in the beginning of the 20th century for the way the body moves in an expressive manner are the underpinnings of modern dance. This chapter outlines those principles, which involve an understanding of space, time, weight, and flow. With these ideas as the foundation, this chapter also covers the five most common movement principles seen in modern dance: central initiation, breath, integrated body, a preference for flow over shape, and countertension. The chapter concludes with a description of the basic positions and nonlocomotor and locomotor movements used in modern dance.

To find supplementary materials for this chapter, such as learning activities, e-journal assignments, and web links, visit the web resource at **www.HumanKinetics.com/BeginningModernDance1E.**

5

Basics of Dance Composition

Modern dance, like every form of dance, is not just about producing or perfecting movements but also about making dances. The pioneers of the art form created dances to express themselves as individuals and to reflect changes in society. Many of the dances they choreographed helped to shift the culture as a result. Responding to change in the world and being on the forefront of new trends are what modern dance is about. This means that part of learning to be a modern dancer means reflecting on yourself and the world around you through the creative process. Finding your own artistic and choreographic voice is an important part of connecting to modern dance. Like the forerunners of modern dance, you are your own guide for deciding what you want to make dances about and what those dances will ultimately reflect about you and the society in which you are creating art. This chapter offers some basic tools for making studies and modern dances. A **study** is a practice dance that is choreographed for the purpose of learning to create. It is an experiment into choreography that may later be revised into a dance that is performed, or it could just be a tool for learning. The content or ideas behind these dances will be up to you. Finding your own voice as an artist is a critical part of the modern dance journey, and creating dances is an important step toward that goal.

The steps, techniques, and movements of modern dance were developed so that choreographers could create works of art using a particular vocabulary and style of movement. These movements are structured into dances using a variety of guiding methods. While no two choreographers use exactly the same methods, there are some general elements of the creative process that will help you to understand how to make and view modern dance. The creative process is not one prescribed way to create art. The **creative process** is an exploration in which you attempt to come up with a unique solution to a complex problem.

Modern dance students interact with dance composition in three ways: They can perform in a piece of choreography, create a dance, or view a modern dance. Many modern dance classes culminate in an informal performance in which the instructor can act as choreographer of the dance, or the class members themselves can contribute movement and ideas to the dance. If you have this opportunity, you will have a chance to learn about the creative process in dance from the inside out. This chapter covers the parts of the choreographic process in modern dance, looking at the range of aesthetics in the art form, investigating ways to create and manipulate movement, and examining common structures of dances. More information about viewing modern dance is covered in chapter 6.

> **DID YOU KNOW?** ▶ ▶ ▶ ▶ ▶ ▶ ▶ ▶
>
> The word *choreographer* derives from Greek and means "graphic writer." During the 18th century, the term *choreographer* came into use and replaced earlier terms, such as *dance supervisor* or *arranger*, to mean people who created dances.

CREATIVE PROCESS IN DANCE

Award-winning modern dance choreographer Bill T. Jones defined dance as "action and shape designed in space and time to express feelings and ideas" (Jones & Kuklin 1998, p. 32). Choreography is the process of designing this shape and action of the body. The movement in a dance and its structure or form are generated with a specific intention in choreography; that means the dance is created to produce a certain visual, emotional, or narrative effect. Unlike the combinations of movement that you learn in a dance technique class, which are created to help you gain or review specific physical skills, movement in choreography is created more for how it will be viewed or how it fits with the idea of a dance. The process of creating dances, like all creative acts, is really an ongoing cycle of activities, which involve creating, evaluating, and revising.

Although each artist is unique in her specific strategies, the choreographer generally begins the choreographic process with movement invention or some kind of exploration around an idea. In modern dance, this often includes the dancers' input in the piece. Ways to generate movement for yourself or with other dancers are covered later in this chapter in more detail, but the essential start of the process is the translation of ideas into movement.

The second phase of the creative cycle is evaluation. This is when a choreographer decides whether the dance is following the ideas or aesthetic principles that are the basis of the dance. This is not necessarily a discrete phase of the process but happens continually as the choreographer watches the dancers execute the movements of the dance. Some choreographers use a video of the dance, which they view after the rehearsal to assist with their evaluation. Others use outside dancers or choreographers to act as an outside eye in deciding how the dance should be changed or adapted to be its most effective. Developing your eye for evaluating dance is an important skill for any dancer or choreographer.

The third phase of choreography is the revision of the dance. This could involve changing movement, structures of the dance, use of space, or any of the other elements of dance discussed in chapter 4. Like evaluation, this is not necessarily a separate activity, but it could happen continually throughout the process. Lots of changes and adaptations will take place as movement is being created as well as after the dance is mostly complete. Some choreographers make rough drafts of the dance and then make major changes in structure afterward; other choreographers make changes along the way and only small changes at the end of the process. This is because the creation of dances is really a repetitive series of creating, evaluating, and revising. This cycle can happen many times as the dance is being made. Each artist repeats these steps in his or her own way until the dance reflects the ideas and values of the choreographer.

AESTHETIC PRINCIPLES

Aesthetic means beauty, and aesthetic preferences refer to what is considered beautiful in the context of modern dance. Since modern dance is not one style of dance, rather an umbrella term that covers several distinct styles of related dance forms, there is not one definition of beauty in modern dance. A beautiful dance may be one that is meaningful although not necessarily pleasing or entertaining to watch. A few elements are common among all forms of dance; these are the five aesthetic elements of unity, balance, variety, repetition and contrast, as well as abstract and narrative symbols. These ideas are important in technique class and also shape modern dance choreography.

The five elements that contribute to the beauty of a piece are referred to as **aesthetic principles**. Aesthetic principles are the fundamental ideas of beauty or sensory satisfaction that people hold about an object or a work of art. These are one way to evaluate the success of a piece of choreography. Keep in mind that what constitutes beautiful is quite different from dance to dance and from artist to artist. If the dance is about a challenging or confrontational topic, it may not be pleasing to watch, but it could still be aesthetically successful. The following five aesthetic principles of dance are present to a certain degree in every piece of choreography. How a choreographer chooses to use them varies from dance to dance.

Modern dance classes often include the chance to learn choreography.

Unity

Unity is the idea of cohesiveness or consistency in a work. A dance that has a great deal of unity, for example, may be a dance that has a theme that is carried throughout the work. Unity can also refer to the idea that all of the components of the dance feel connected for the viewer. The four succeeding aesthetic elements contribute to the unity of a dance.

Balance

Balance usually refers to an equal or logical treatment of rest and action in a work. A balanced work has intense moments that are contrasted with more sedate moments. The balance of elements gives the audience a chance to absorb both the intensity and quiet of the dance. Balance can also refer to the use of space in a dance. Symmetry is not required in a balanced work, but the choreographer must show an awareness of using the space in a satisfying and meaningful way.

Variety

Variety means using many types of movements and shapes in a dance. A dance with variety uses not only a lot of different steps but also a number of facings for the dancers, variety in the number of dancers on stage at the same time, variation in tempo (speeds in the dance), several formation changes, and differing intensities in performance energy.

Repetition

Repeating phrases of movement, formations in the dance, or any other choreographic element is a part of the construction of every dance. **Repetition** can make a dance more cohesive and help the audience recognize important sections of the dance. A choreographer must be skillful in using repetition so that a dance balances familiar material with new material. This is the counterpart to variety. Both are necessary for an aesthetically successful modern dance.

Contrast

Contrast refers to the moments when a choreographer makes a movement stand out because it is very different in some way from the rest of the dance or by juxtaposing two different movements against each another. These highlights can add a lot of excitement and meaning to a work and keep it from becoming too predictable for an audience.

MEANING MAKING

Each form of dance has its own way of making meaning. The preceding aesthetic principles of unity, balance, variety, repetition, and contrast all lead to meaning making in a dance. The making of meaningful dance leads to beauty. A powerful, meaningful dance may not be pretty in the traditional sense, but its very ability to make you think and feel is a thing of beauty. The aesthetics of modern dance vary widely from style to style within the genre. For some styles, an aesthetically successful dance is one that is beautiful in its design and execution. For other styles, a truly successful dance will be one that portrays a powerful emotion or conveys a clear idea to the audience. For many dances it is the interplay of the various aesthetic elements that makes a work powerful or successful. Chapter 8 explains in further detail the specific aesthetics of five of the major styles of modern

> **ACTIVITY** ▶▶▶▶▶▶▶▶▶▶
>
> ### Meet Your Modern Dance Muse
>
> Stand in the center of a space and visualize a dancer performing in front of you with clarity and confidence. Follow that dancer and perform his or her movement.

dance: Graham, Humphrey-Limón, Cunningham, Horton, and Dunham. These preferences will further help you interpret and evaluate modern dance when you see it performed, an activity you will practice in chapter 6. Fulfilling the specific aesthetic requirements of each style will take some time to develop as you and your teacher better identify the style, or combination of styles, of modern dance that you are learning.

CHOREOGRAPHIC TECHNIQUES

The beginning of the choreographic process is the development of a movement idea. Ideas for dances can come from anywhere. Something happening in your life, a book you have read, a painting, an interesting gesture or movement—the possibilities are endless. Choreographers use many techniques to create and refine movement so that it best expresses the ideas they want to explore or communicate. Most of these techniques begin with improvisation and continue into motif development.

Improvisation

Improvisation is the spontaneous creation of movement. This means that you are inventing the movement as you do it. When you hear a song you like and begin to move to it, you are improvising. Playing, letting go, acting on impulse, listening, and trusting yourself are all part of the improvisation process. Very often improvisation in dance is structured around a movement task or an idea. For example, you might be asked to improvise for a certain number of counts during the combination at the end of class, with the guidelines that you travel low to the floor or move in a circular path. This same idea of structuring improvisational exercises can be used as a very satisfying way to dance in and of itself, but it is also often used as a way to generate movement to be used in choreography. Some choreographers improvise movement for themselves and then teach the material to the dancers. Other choreographers improvise with their dancers during rehearsal. The movement you create during the rehearsal process may be shaped and used in the choreography itself. This is frequently true in modern dance where it is common for a choreographer to highlight the individuality and specific talents of the performers. Some common improvisational structures are suggested in the following section to help you with your investigations, but this is by no means a comprehensive list. Your teacher will have many other strategies to help you develop movement ideas.

Moving From Visual Images

Photographs, paintings, sculptures, and videos can inspire movement creation. Pick an image that resonates with you or with the idea you want to make a dance about. If there is a spatial pattern evident in the visual art you have selected, begin to move in the space in that same pattern. Allow yourself many repetitions of the pattern and see how the movement naturally alters or adapts as you move. Perhaps there is a central figure or object in the image. Embody the shape of that figure or object. Allow yourself to respond to the position your body is in. Unfold the position, move one body part, or try the position standing, seated, lying on the floor, or traveling through space. Make a list of emotions that the art evokes for you. Move to each of these emotional states using the patterns or shapes you found in the artwork.

Moving From Words

Language can be a powerful force in motivating dance. You can work from a list of words—perhaps ones that suggest action, such as a list of words with –ing endings—or a text such as a poem or a monologue. Listen to the language as you read the text out loud. If it contains a rhythm, begin to move to the rhythm of the words. Try putting this rhythm in just one part of your body, such as your legs. Shift the rhythm to your arms or your hips as you continue to improvise. Make a list of the images in the text. Let these images guide your movements as you did with visual art images. Find the most meaningful words in the text. Describe the quality that these words have for you in movement terms. In other words, do these words suggest moving sharply, slowly, or low to the ground? Use these as qualities or guidelines for inventing movement.

Tasks

Improvisation can also be based on a specific task or assignment. For example, move from one corner of the space to the opposite corner of the space beginning low and ending as high up from the floor as you can. Or move in a circular pattern in the space, but begin movements only with your left foot. Perhaps select a body part from which to begin traveling in the space. If you want to change direction, you must begin with a different body part. A common improvisational task requires dancers to move on a grid pattern on the floor, making only 90-degree turns in the space. Any task like this can lead you to moving in new ways that you haven't tried before and help you to develop movement ideas.

Senses

People experience life through the five senses of seeing, hearing, tasting, touching, and smelling. Pick any one of these senses as a motivation for improvisation. Eat a bit of sweet chocolate. Respond with movement to the sensation. Now eat a bitter piece of dark chocolate. See if your body responds with movement in the same way. Smell perfume wafting in the air. Let this inspire your movement. Feel an ice cube and respond to the cold using your torso. Sensory experiences are rich with the possibility of bodily response.

Responding to Someone Else

Improvisation does not need to be done solo. In fact, it is quite often a group activity. You can respond to the movement of others in the space with you. You can alternate moving with another dancer, for example, as if you are in dialogue with him. Just like a conversation with words, your movement response is shaped by how your partner moves. If he moves toward you, you can respond by coming even closer or moving away. You can learn a movement from another dancer and change it by adding to it or deleting from it. You can sculpt the shape of another dancer's body and move in the negative spaces created by your partner's position.

There are as many ways to improvise movement as there are ideas for dances. Whatever stimulates you to make movement that suits your dance is an appropriate starting point. The more time you can give to moving without judging yourself, the more original your movement will tend to be. Improvisation should be like a structured play session where your body indulges in the creative process.

ACTIVITY ▶▶▶▶▶ ▶▶ ▶ ▶▶▶▶

Improvisation

Say your full name (first, middle, and last) out loud and clap to each syllable. Now move just your arms to this rhythm. Next, move just your legs to the same beat pattern. Move your whole body to this rhythm. Move across the space to the rhythm pattern. You have been improvising! See if there are movements you just created that you would like to repeat and teach to someone else.

Motif and Phrase Development

The movement material that is created during improvisation, after some refinement, is often referred to as a **motif**. This term means a small section of movement that expresses a central idea or theme of the dance. Once a choreographer has a motif or several motifs started for a dance, she develops the motif into phrase material. A motif is a movement idea, while a **movement phrase** is a sentence of dance or a grouping of meaningful movements. Often the development of the motifs and movement phrases help a dance to become more coherent or more in line with the most frequently observed aesthetics of modern dance. The following techniques for motif and phrase development will help you to create material that shows the principles of variety, repetition, and contrast in your choreography. These techniques are not comprehensive. They are simply common methods that you might find useful in your creative journey. Many of these are similar to the way in which musicians develop musical phrases.

Repetition

Just as it sounds, **repetition** means to repeat all or parts of a movement phrase or motif. This can be a very useful tool, particularly if different dancers repeat different parts of the motif or movement phrase. A sense of both variety and unity can be achieved with this technique. When you watch the work of famous choreographers, look for what parts of the dance are repeated. This is often a clue to spotting the most significant movement motifs in a piece of choreography.

Embellishment

The technique of **embellishment** means to elaborate on a phrase by making changes in aspects of the movement. This generally means accenting, or highlighting, certain parts of the phrase. This can be done in numerous ways—adding a pause or stillness into the combination, doing some movements with sharper or smoother dynamics, adding a turn or a roll to the floor. Some of the following techniques could be used as ways to embellish a movement motif.

Augmentation and Diminution

Augmentation means to add on to a phrase of movement; **diminution** means to make a phrase smaller. Movement motifs can be augmented, or enlarged, with new movement or with repetition. Dance phrases can be made smaller by deleting elements or performing only parts of the movement.

> ### ACTIVITY ▶▶▶▶▶▶▶▶▶▶▶▶
> ## Phrase Development
> Begin with 16 counts of movement that you know well. Teach it to two dancers. Have the dancers perform it for you, both facing forward. Now have the dancers perform the phrase of dance with one dancer facing backward and one facing forward. How does this change the effect of the dance for you? Try this again with the dancers facing in two different directions of your choice. How does this variety add to the movement?

Splicing

Splicing refers to inserting different or new material into the existing movement motifs. This could be material that the individual performer creates and inserts into the movement or could be something the choreographer chooses to add from another source.

Change of Facing

Facing refers to how the dance is oriented with respect to the space. While dancers often learn dance phrases while facing the mirror or the front of the room, you can perform movements facing any direction. You can turn the entire movement motif to face the back, side, or corners of the stage. You will notice that dances by professional modern dance choreographers frequently have dancers doing the same movement at the same time but facing in different directions to enhance variety in the choreography.

Change of Level

The level of the movement, or how high or low it is from the floor, can dramatically change the look of a movement phrase. Adapting the movement so that some dancers do the movement standing and others do it seated on the floor would radically alter the look of a movement motif.

Change of Timing

The **tempo** of the movement, or speed at which it is performed, can be varied within a phrase of dance. Performing some sections of the phrase more slowly while other sections are performed faster might highlight some element of the motif or a specific movement within it. The same movement combination could be performed quickly by some dancers and slowly by other dancers, or at different tempos at different points in the dance.

Change of Body Part

Similar to the way composers can change the sound of a phrase of music by changing what instrument plays it (for example, the same melody played on a tuba and a violin would sound quite different), so a choreographer can change what part of the body does a movement. A movement motif in which the arms extend alternately overhead would be vastly changed if that same movement were performed by the legs kicking upward alternately while the dancer lies on his back on the floor. A small clapping gesture with the hands could be performed with the elbows or forearms to increase variety in the choreography.

CHOREOGRAPHIC STRUCTURES

Choreographic structure refers to the architecture of a dance. This is the overall framework for creating the dance that organizes the motifs and phrases that you develop. Decisions that each choreographer must make about the number of dancers in a work, whether the central idea is to tell a story or to focus on abstract imagery,

A larger dance often includes smaller group work within it.

whether the dance will be performed the same way each time, or whether it will include elements of improvisation or chance all fall into this category. Sometimes choreographers decide the structure of the dance before developing any movement material; other times choreographers play with developing movement and then create a structure that best fits the movement ideas being developed.

Solo, Duet, or Group

One of the main structural decisions you will need to make about any dance you are creating is the number of dancers in the piece. Any idea can be explored through any format, but dances that result from solo structures are very different from those that result from large-group dances. The principles of motif development are the same, but other choreographic elements, particularly relating to the use of **unison** (everyone moving together doing the same thing at the same time) and **counterpoint** (dancers on stage doing different things at the same time), come into play with group choreography, even groups as small as a duet. Remember also that a solo, duet, trio, or quartet can be a section of a larger group dance, allowing a choreographer to use more than one structure in a dance.

Use of Narrative and Abstract Symbols

Because modern dance is really a more general term for several styles of choreography, the genre embraces using both narrative and abstract symbols to express itself. The narrative use of symbols is when the choreographer attempts to tell a story or create theatrical characters in a dance. An abstract use of symbols occurs when the metaphors in the dance are not connected to a story but may be based on creating a mood, design, or other less direct means of communicating to the audience. Some choreographers prefer one way of creating dances to another; others use both symbolic methods. Choreographers may use a synthesized approach sometimes referred to as an abstract narrative, where there is no specific characterization developed in the dancers, but a loose narrative is apparent in the choreography. Modern dance is open to many ways of meaning making through choreography.

Narrative Symbols

Many modern dances have stories to tell. Several dances of modern dance pioneer Martha Graham are retellings of classical myths, such as the story of Oedipus Rex, which is featured in *Night Journey* (1947) and *Clytemnestra* (1958). In a narrative modern dance, dancers are portrayed as specific characters, and the ideas behind the dance are revealed as the dancers interact and express each character's state of mind. Many times these kinds of modern dances will have sets and costumes that help communicate the time period of the story and the identities of the dancers' characters. Although the movements the dancers will do in a narrative modern dance look different than in a classical ballet, the idea of storytelling using the body is the same. Narrative storytelling in modern dance, however, does not have to be an overt or obvious storyline. In some narratives, or more specifically abstract narratives, the story of the dance is open to interpretation.

Abstract Symbols

Modern in the term *modern dance* does not mean new or contemporary. Modern, in this context, reflects the modernist movement in art from the early part of the 20th century. So named because it was new at the time, this movement in art explored the use of abstract symbol making. Modern dance has held on to this quality. Much of the art form uses the body as an abstract instrument of expression rather than as a theatrical character for storytelling. This means that while a narrative dance uses the body as a human dramatic character, an abstract dance uses the body more as a shape in space. From this perspective, the body or multiple bodies in modern dance are seen as creating patterns made out of the body's shapes and the spaces around the body. The design of movements in an abstract modern dance is based on creating meaningful positive and negative shapes with the body in space and effective composition of the spaces on the stage. Curve the middle of your body back so that your spine makes a C-shape and curve your arms in front of you as if you are holding something large and round in front of you. Modern dance is concerned not only with the C-shape of your body but also with the ball, or sphere, of empty space that is carved out of the air in front of you. This ball is the negative space created by your body; the C-shape of your body is the positive space.

When the body is viewed abstractly in modern dance, it does not mean it is not conveying meaning or emotion and is merely an interesting shape. On the contrary, abstract modern dances are frequently concerned with issues of humanity and human existence. A modern dance choreographer wanting to express the stresses of modern life through dance could have the dancers portray a series of characters whose interactions are imitative of a hectic lifestyle. This is an example of narrative symbol making. Equally valid in modern dance is to crowd the stage with dancers moving furiously in all directions with no recognizable pedestrian actions as a symbol of our busy and disconnected modern life. This is an abstract communication of the same theme.

Symbolic meaning making does not mean that the symbols in modern dance are universal. There is no fixed meaning associated with any particular movement of the body. A jump can mean joy in one piece, despair in another, and simply the use of energy in yet another. How you interpret the symbols or images you see in a dance depends on the context of the dance and your own experiences in life and in watching dance. No two audience members get exactly the same meaning from a piece of modern choreography, and this is considered normal—frequently desired—in modern dance.

Collage

Many modern dances are created in much the same way that visual artists create collages. In visual art, a collage is an assemblage of mixed media, often including found objects. In dance, a piece of choreography can be created in a similar fashion. Assorted material from the dancers themselves, or other sources, is put together by the choreographer to create one cohesive whole. One of these sources, or found elements, could be improvisation. Sometimes a choreographer will structure a section of a dance so that the dancers can make decisions about movement choices during the performance. This can add to the focus of the performers and the liveliness of the performance.

Chance

Modern dancer and choreographer Merce Cunningham was famous for the use of chance operations in his choreography. Not to be confused with improvisation, chance is a way to structure set movement material. For example, a choreographer could create eight movement phrases, each identified by a number, that the dancers learn completely. The choreographer would then put the numbers 1 through 8 on slips of paper, put them in a hat, and pull them out one by one. The dance would then consist of performing the movement phrases in the order in which they came out of the hat. This could be done once, and then the dance is set, or this could be done every night before the performance. Many variables in a dance can be decided by chance, if this is your method, from the order of the movement phrases to the number of dancers performing or the direction that the dancers will face during the performance. The movement itself is

ACTIVITY ▸▸▸▸▸▸ ▸ ▸▸▸▸▸▸

Chance Operations

Get together with a partner. Each of you creates 8 counts of movement. Teach each other your phrase. Now roll one die. Whatever number it lands on will be the number of times you do your phrase in the dance. Roll the die again. This number will be the number of times you do your partner's 8-count phrase. See how the chance roll of a die affects your dance study.

set and not improvised, but the forces of random chance will affect the overall look and structure of the choreography.

CHOREOGRAPHIC FORMS

After you decide on the overall structure of the dance, you can use certain common forms to build the dance itself. Form is also the way the motifs and phrases you have developed fit together to create the overall structure of the dance. These could be the same as the structure of the music, but many times in modern dance the form of the dance and the form of the music are different. The first three forms explained here (AB or ABA, rondo, and theme and variations) come from the vocabulary of music, but they are a guide to several possibilities in structuring your choreography; they do not need to be based on the music you are using, if you are using music at all.

AB or ABA

This form means that there are two parts to the dance, section A and section B, which are different from each other. These distinct sections are usually related in some way, like a sunrise section and a sunset section. The dance either is made of two sections or the first section is repeated again at the end of the dance in the **ABA form**. This is a very common format.

> **ACTIVITY** ▶▶▶▶▶▶▶▶▶▶▶▶
>
> ### ABA Form
>
> Get together with a partner. Each of you creates a 16-count phrase of movement. Teach each other your phrases. Perform your phrase first, then your partner's, and then yours again. You have created a short study in the ABA form.onal.

Rondo

The **rondo** form is common in popular music and is roughly like a verse-and-chorus structure. A phrase or small section A is repeated in between new sections B, C, D, and so on. The traditional rondo form has at least three verses and ends with the familiar A section, making the piece structure ABACADA. This could be expanded for as long as the choreographer wants.

Theme and Variations

As the title suggests, in **theme and variation** the choreographer develops a thematic phrase or movement material. The piece progresses by altering or varying the original phrase. This usually happens several times over the course of the dance so that the form looks like A, A1, A2, A3, A4, and so on. The choreographic devices involved in motif development could be a guide for developing these variations.

Natural Forms

Depending on the idea behind your dance, the form of the choreography may follow a pattern found in nature as opposed to an external structure like those listed previously. Common configurations of **natural forms** include following the four seasons, tracking a life cycle from young to old, or other natural progressions in life.

The form of your dance is one more element that will support your communication through movement. Be sure to experiment with various forms so that the overall structure of your dance makes an effective statement and enhances the movements and motifs you have created.

SUMMARY

Creating dances is often a part of learning modern dance. While each artist has his own unique creative process, most involve invention, evaluation, and revision. For most forms of modern dance, this process will be guided by five aesthetic principles: unity, balance, variety, repetition, and contrast. To choreograph dances that follow these principles to make meaning, you can employ a variety of techniques. Many of these techniques begin with improvisation to create movement motifs. These motifs or phrases can be developed using a variety of methods, such as repetition; embellishment; and change of facing, timing, or body part. Once movement material has been developed, or as the material is being created, you as the choreographer can decide on an overall structure for the dance, determining how many dancers will perform, how abstract or narrative the piece may be, and whether it will include chance or movement material from sources other than you. Within the larger architecture of the dance, you will use one of many choreographic forms, which help to structure the movement. These forms can be based on musical forms or language forms, such as ABA, rondo, and theme and variation, or other natural forms such as the passage of time. The choreographic process in modern dance can be a vehicle for finding your artistic voice, enhancing your experience with the art form, and supporting your experiences in technique class.

To find supplementary materials for this chapter, such as learning activities, e-journal assignments, and web links, visit the web resource at **www.HumanKinetics.com/BeginningModernDance1E.**

6

Performing and Responding to Modern Dance

Many dancers take dance classes because it is fun and challenging. Going to technique class is a rewarding activity in and of itself, but many dancers also take classes in the hopes of performing modern dance. You might have a chance to do this during or at the end of the term in an informal showing in the dance studio or in performance testing as part of your technique class. You might also get the chance to be in a more formal performance setting in a theater, since many high schools and colleges have student dance companies that perform modern dance. Whether or not you become a performer, many dance classes require you to attend a performance of a professional modern dance company or a college or university dance company in a theater. The connections between learning the technique in the dance studio and viewing a performance or performing in a theater are important ones. As you have already learned, modern dance technique was developed to train dancers for performance as well as reap the rewards of class participation.

This chapter looks at how you can prepare for performance testing in the classroom and informal and formal performances through your technique class. You will look at ways of remembering movement and ways to enjoy the performing experience. This chapter also guides you in getting the most out of viewing live professional dance.

LEARNING MOVEMENT FOR PERFORMANCE

Learning movement to perform is essentially the same as learning any movement in class. It is still necessary to learn the sequence of the movements, where they originate in the body, where they move in space, the rhythm or timing of the movement, and the quality with which the movements should be performed. The biggest difference is how long you will need to retain the movement sequences. Some instructors repeat sequences and build on them each class; others present new material each time. If you have a teacher who builds on previously taught material, then you are on the way to acquiring the skill of remembering dance sequences already. There are several habits, however, that you can develop that will help you with remembering dances for performance.

Developing a Visual Memory

Your **visual memory** is the ability to remember what you see. This is an important part of both performing and responding to modern dance. As a participant in choreography, you will need to learn to see sequences of movement and repeat them. One way to develop your visual memory is to create an internal monologue, or narration of what is going on. As you are doing the movements, you may want to talk yourself through the movements by finding word cues. A sentence of dance in your head might sound like "Run, leap, turn, slide, go to floor." Sometimes your teacher will say these cues out loud in class. These word cues will help to develop your memory for what you see, because they will help you to put the movements together into units or phrases. You do not need to know the actual names of the steps to do this. Use word cues that are meaningful to you.

> **TECHNIQUE TIP** ▶▶▶▶▶▶▶▶▶▶
>
> Remembering the sequence of movements and visualizing the combination are vital to learning the combination. Saying action words that describe the movement to yourself is another way to remember the combination. Repeating these words while you run the images of the movement sequence in your head strings together the movements.

Note Taking

In your academic classes in high school or college, you have undoubtedly gotten into the habit of taking notes. The act of writing down your thoughts makes it easier to remember them. The same is true for dance. Writing down what you have learned will help you to remember it, even if you don't have a lot of time to study what you have written. You should record notes as close to the end of class as possible so that your memory is fresh. This can become one of the most productive habits you develop in your dance life. In this way, you will be training your memory as well as your body and spirit through dance. Several methods for note taking on dance are available in the web resource that accompanies this text.

> ## ACTIVITY ▶▶▶▶▶ ▶▶▶▶▶
>
> ## Taking Notes
>
> Immediately after your next modern dance class, take notes on the across-the-floor combination. The next day, try to recall that sequence of movements. Now look at your notes and see if it easier to remember the choreography.

Once you have taken notes immediately after the class or rehearsal, be sure to review the notes within 24 hours. This will ensure that your notes are comprehensible to you. As you gain temporal distance from an event, you tend to remember only the larger picture or the most poignant features of an event, not necessarily the details. Right after class, jot down an outline of what you want to remember and fill it out more completely, or add key words or images, the next day as you review.

Focusing on the Rudiments: What, Where, When, With Whom

Whether you are learning movement for a performance or a performance testing situation, you should focus on some questions that will help you to not only learn the material but also remember it longer and perform it more confidently. The first level of your attention should focus on the rudiments of the dance, which will help you with learning and remembering choreography.

These rudiments include knowing what, where, when, and with whom. *What* refers to the actual steps you are expected to execute. You should focus, for example, on whether the leap is done with a straight leg or a bent leg, whether the turn is on the right foot or the left, and whether the arm is straight or slightly curved. *Where* refers to the spatial dimension of the combination or choreography. It is possible that the dance studio where you rehearse will be of different dimensions than the stage or dance studio where you will do your performance testing, so it is important to know where you are relative to the space. For example, you might remember you are one quarter of the way across the room, no matter what the exact size of the room is. *When* refers to the timing of the piece. You will need to notice whether you enter based on a musical cue, such as a count of the music or when a particular part of the music is played, or if you are coming in based on a visual cue, such as another dancer exiting or moving downstage. Along with *where*, *with whom* is a useful thing to note. It is probable that not everyone in the combination or study will be doing the same things, so it will be important to pay attention to who is dancing each section with you. You can rely on your fellow dancers to be not only spatial landmarks, but also a good resource for practice. There is a unique connection between dancers performing in a piece of choreography. The nonverbal communication that you share with a fellow performer is a special kind of shared energy. Be sure to appreciate this opportunity to connect with other people.

Expanding Your Focus: How and Why

Beginning dancers often make the mistake of concentrating all their energy on what they are supposed to do. When they have mastered the what, where, when, and with whom, they feel they know the work. Many choreographers, from your classmates to the masters, however, make dances because they want to communicate an idea or inspire a response from the audience. This means that the how and why of the combination, study, or dance are important to know and express in addition to simply knowing what you are doing. It is true that for most dances the teacher or choreographer has put a lot of the intention of the piece into the elements of movement vocabulary, structure of the dance, and use of space, but the performance quality that the dancers bring to a work is still an important factor in any dance's ability to communicate. This means you will need to focus on the *how* and the *why* of the dance. *How* refers to the quality that you will use in approaching the movement phrases. Even in everyday life, you imbue movements with a quality. If you are walking across the room to greet someone you haven't seen in a long time, you will walk with a certain energy and openness in the body. If you cross that same space to see a person who has angered you, you might display a more powerful body posture and your feet may strike the floor more forcefully. You are still doing the same *what* of walking, the same *where* of across the room, and the same *when* of moving to a person when he enters, but the *how* of your movement will be different. If you are unsure of the *how* of a movement phrase, ask the teacher. The answer to your question will be helpful to everyone participating in the piece or class combination.

The *how* that guides the way you perform a piece is usually based on the *why* element of a dance. Some dances tell a story, so the *why* you are doing a certain movement is often tied to communicating a character or an emotional response. Some studies or combinations communicate a feeling, so the *why* element will be more about embodying the emotion so that the idea can be made visible to the audience. Some dances, particularly those prepared for informal class showings, are created to showcase your growing skills as a dancer. In this case, the *why* may be to show off a particular movement or encourage you to learn a new way of moving. If you can't tell why a movement or element of a dance is part of the choreography, then it is likely the audience will not be able to see it, either. Watch the rehearsal video your teacher posts for you and see if you can find the *why*. If it is not obvious after viewing, be sure to inquire. You are helping the choreographer if you ask reasonable questions after you have done your best to perfect what she requires of you.

Practicing Choreography

Class time is important for learning and practicing choreography, but it is not the only time that you should practice. A serious dancer reviews choreography between classes or rehearsals. Not everyone has a space to do this. Fortunately, there are

Practicing a dance is a way to learn movement and connect to the group.

two good ways to rehearse a dance without a large studio space. In fact, these can be done in the hall outside of the studio or in your room. The first of these ways is to reread your rehearsal notes. This will remind you of the movement that was covered last time and perhaps even some of the ideas of how you should perform the movement. You can review your notes alone, or you can do this with another dancer in the piece. If you are all warming up together outside the studio, reviewing notes is a good way to conclude your warm-up sequence.

The second way to rehearse without the space of the studio is to mark the sequences of the piece. **Marking** is a term used to mean doing the dance in a very small way. You indicate the movements rather than execute them fully (for example, bending slightly instead of going all the way to the floor, or doing mostly the arm movements instead of involving your whole back). This is an excellent way to solidify your memory of a sequence of movement. Often a dancer marking a dance outside the studio will be joined by other dancers from the same piece. Marking is a good skill to have, since you might need to employ it when you are tired or injured as well. You can review the emotions and qualities of a dance, even if you are marking the movements and spacing. Many dancers review their choreography by listening to the music for the dance and visualizing themselves in the dance as the music plays. Several more techniques for reviewing dances are covered in the web resource that accompanies this text.

Calming Exercises Before Performing

Every performer is different, but most have some preshow nerves. Even for informal showings, some dancers are more worried than others. If you are one of those dancers, you can do certain things to relax before you perform. No matter what method you use, remember that just about everyone feels the way you do, and some preperformance anxiety can give you the energy for an excellent performance.

The key is in not letting your nerves get the better of you and allowing yourself to actually enjoy the experience of performing for others. For many dancers, the performance is the icing on the cake. The contrast between the preshow nerves and the exhilaration of performing and the wonderful sense of accomplishment that follows can be a fulfilling, even addicting, experience.

There are three common techniques for relaxing before a performance. No one way works for every dancer. If you get the chance to speak with someone you respect as a performer, ask her how she deals with this issue. She may have a solution that you could try. One common technique is to control your breathing. When you are nervous, your heart rate and breathing become faster. Slow this down with deep, even breaths. The act of calming your body physically will have a powerful effect, since mind and body are so closely linked. Often dancers refer to controlling their breathing and feeling calm and capable as a result as centering themselves.

The second technique for dealing with nervous energy is to distract yourself by stretching or marking through the dance. The effect of small physical movements will relax the tensions that you hold in your muscles. Be careful not to overdo the stretches or the run-through of choreography, which can make you susceptible to injury.

A third technique for chasing away stage fright is to focus on an image or an inspiration. Imagining the character that you are about to portray in a dance or putting yourself in the mood that the dance will convey can focus your mental energy and concentration in the performance. Look around you and take in the environment. Seeing the other performers and feeling the connection that exists between you as collaborators in the artistic process will help you to enjoy the experience and realize what an amazing adventure you are a part of. The ability to see the bigger picture of the performance and the perspective that dance is not about individual steps but collective experience can be comforting. You might also consider focusing mentally on a quotation from a writer you find inspirational or the advice of a well-known choreographer. A list of motivating preshow quotations can be found in the web resource.

VIEWING AND RESPONDING TO MODERN DANCE PERFORMANCES

While you are studying modern dance in the studio, you should take the opportunity to see live professional modern dance. Many students may not live in communities where live dance is available or affordable. If professional modern dance companies do not come to your community, several online videos and commercial DVDs are available for viewing professional dance. It is important to see professional dancers performing. Many popular dance shows are on television, but most are focused on amateurs competing. No matter how good the amateurs, the dancers in a professional company have a connection to the choreographer and special training in the technique they are performing that is different from any other kind of performance. It is important as a dancer to develop a sense of the aesthetics of each kind of modern dance style you may encounter. Seeing a live professional performance is an invaluable resource for developing your understanding of the art form of modern dance.

Many colleges and universities have excellent student dance companies. Support your peers by watching their performances. Many of these companies perform reconstructions of historical masterworks and perform the original works of current artists as well. The long-standing tradition of college dance ensemble performances is one worth viewing.

In fact, it is likely that you will be required to watch live professional dance, if it is available in your area, or you will need to see dance on video or attend the college dance group's performance as a part of your dance class. Your instructor will also likely require you to discuss or write a response to your viewing experience. The following are guidelines on how to do this response.

If you haven't had a lot of experience with viewing modern dance, you may be hesitant to interpret the dances you are seeing. Just remember that there is no absolute right and wrong in responding to a dance. You may even have a different response to a dance each time you watch it, depending on your mood or experiences. True masterwork dances are often valued because they are so rich and in depth that it is possible to see many aspects in them over many viewings. The best approach is to keep an open mind and write about or discuss what you see. Writing helps to clarify your thoughts. As you commit words to paper, your mind becomes engaged in deeper analysis. Rereading your thoughts as you write can also help to shed light on your response. Similarly, if you have the chance to discuss the work with someone else, you will find that you know more about what you saw than you think. Explaining what you observed is a great practice for describing movement, an activity that will help you to learn movements more quickly. If you are trying to discuss a dance with someone else, you will be tempted to describe the images that you saw rather than describe every step. This is also a good practice for interpreting what you see.

Neither the writing nor the discussion will be productive in understanding a work of art if you only discuss what you think the artist's intention was. Discuss what you saw in the work, whether or not that matches what you think you were supposed to see. A dance can be like a text. Your reading of it should be based on the text itself, not a critic's interpretation. It is fine to read what others have said about a dance, but be sure you have your own thoughts as well.

After you see a dance, you will be asked to write a **reflection**, or respond to what you saw. This could be in the form of a written evaluation, an informal journal reflection, or a class discussion. The process of writing can help to clarify your thinking about a dance. There are many ways to create a written

DID YOU KNOW? ▶▶▶▶▶▶▶

Dance pioneer Ted Shawn was inspired to become a dancer because he saw a live professional performance of early modern dancer Ruth St. Denis. Live performance can inspire you, too!

response to a performance, and your instructor will give you specific guidelines to follow. Following is an explanation of the components of dance writing: describing, analyzing, and evaluating. Describing dance refers to delineating the elements or structures of the dance, such as the number of dancers in the piece, the type of music accompanying it, and the kind of movement the dancers do. Analyzing dance is taking it a step further and making a judgment about what the dance means to you as an observer. This is where you explain, for example, what you think the dance was about, or what the imagery in the dance seemed to communicate. Evaluating dance means giving your opinion about whether the dance was successful or effective. The description and analysis of a dance are the evidence for your evaluation of the work. Simply offering an opinion about whether you liked a particular dance leaves out the most critical thinking about a work, which is describing what you saw and analyzing what it meant to you. This gives context and validity to your opinion.

Description

No matter what form your response takes, you will need to describe what you saw. Description should be in a neutral voice. Describing a dance as "a boring duet with annoying music" is not really a description; it is an opinion or evaluation of a dance. The description of a dance provides common ground for the reader and you the writer to identify the elements of the dance under discussion and what led you to the conclusion you may have drawn about its meaning. Following are several elements that you can use as a checklist when you write about or describe a dance, but be sure to check with your teacher to determine which of these elements are the most critical for you to include in your paper or journal.

Artists' Names

When you write about a dance, credit or record the names of the choreographers, dancers, lighting designer, costume designer, and composer. A work of art cannot be separated entirely from its creators. Their experiences and aesthetic sense are what gave birth to the work. Be sure to give all the artists the respect of including their names in your writing.

Genre or Movement Vocabulary

This refers to the steps of the dance and their general style. This could be a classical vocabulary or lots of movement on the floor. See if you find contractions of the torso or repeated balances in the dance. Describe the general look of the piece and possibly the specific style of modern dance if you can identify it.

Music

Ask yourself how the music is used in the dance. Perhaps it is not playing throughout, and there are moments of silence. Possibly the dancers are not dancing to the rhythm of the music, but it supports the general mood of the piece. Describe what kind of music is used, either by general description (such as classical music) or by instrumentation (such as a guitar solo). Perhaps the music is a sound score or the reading of a text. Be sure to note this as well.

Dancers

While it seems like an obvious item to identify, many dancers write about group dances without really quantifying whether it is a group of 4 or a group of 20 dancers. The dancers in a dance work can participate in choreography in a solo, duet, trio, or other groups. The specific number is not so critical, but offer the reader a general idea of how the dance looked on stage.

Structure and Sequence

Structure, when it relates to dance, refers to the parts in a dance. Sequence refers to the order of the parts of the dance. For example, the dance may begin with a solo dancer in the middle of the stage, who is then joined by a large group of dancers from stage left. This might be where you would describe whether everyone is moving in unison or whether there are several simultaneous solos. These kinds of descriptions give an outline of what happens in the dance. When you practice this kind of description, you begin to notice more about dance structures.

Movement Description

In describing the movement vocabulary, you describe the type of dance it is generally, but it is also necessary to describe some of the specific movements that you see in the dance. The movement descriptions become the evidence for your interpretations of the images in the dance. You must first explain what you saw so that later you can define what the movements meant to you. There are practices in describing movements on the web resource.

Costumes, Set, and Lighting Design

In addition to the design of the dancers' movement and placement in space, other visual design elements can be present in a dance, such as costumes, set, and lighting design. When you write about a dance performance, you do not need to describe the costumes in detail, but thought and artistry are behind the costuming. The costumer collaborated with the choreographer to create a shared vision of the dance. Pay attention to what the costume adds to that vision. Some costumes are very pedestrian, making the dancers appear more human and realistic; other costumes are about color and abstract shape. Take note of whether all the dancers are dressed alike or whether they are each wearing something different. These make very different statements in a dance.

Some modern dances involve sets. A set might have a large ramp or other construction, or it might be a video or slide projections. The set is another designed element to the dance, so you should consider how it helps to communicate the concept behind the dance.

Similarly, the lighting of a dance can make a difference in how a dance is perceived because it helps to direct the viewer's eye around the space. A lighting designer works closely with the choreographer to enhance the mood and spatial relationships that you see on stage.

Video Versus Live Performance

When you write about a video instead of a live performance, you need to be aware of one more element. This is the view of the videographer. While the best way to see a dance on video is often the "archival shot" or "long shot" of a dance, where the camera stays in one place and shoots the whole stage at once, this is rarely the case with professional dance on video. Frequently there are close-ups on dancers' faces, where the videographer has made specific choices or edits in the film you are watching. You do not necessarily need to write about the videographer's contribution to your experience of the dance, but you should take note of it when you watch dance on video, since the film editor or videographer may be giving you his opinion about what is important to view in the choreography.

Analysis

After you have identified or described the critical elements of a dance, the next step of writing is to explain what you saw in the work. This means describing the images, mood, or other impressions you got from seeing the dance. What you see in the dance is based on several personal factors, including your experience in viewing dance and your experience with the topic of the dance, so your analysis is a subjective statement. Although analysis involves opinion, this is still not a place to say that you liked or disliked a dance. Your opinion comes into play because you are describing the images that you saw. These are subject to interpretation. One viewer might see a lonely woman in the solo, yet another sees a defiant pioneer. The images that you see in a work are subjective, but they are still not emotional responses pertaining to liking or disliking a dance. Analysis is taking the elements of the dance that you described and putting them into a context that helps the reader of your paper understand what the dance means to you. Avoid making statements about enjoyment of a dance because your likes and dislikes are only a surface analysis of the work. While it is expected that you will have an emotional response to a dance, understanding and training yourself to describe the features of the artwork that caused your reaction will develop your understanding and appreciation of dance as an art form. The three most basic parts of analysis are interpreting the mood of the piece, the images you see in the work, and the overall metaphor of the work. Examples of dance analysis also appear on the web resource.

Artist's Intention

Many people believe that the point of watching a dance is to get the message that the choreographer intended to communicate. While some dances deliberately tell a story, most modern dances are not quite so direct. The choreographer of a modern dance piece has an initial idea to explore through the creative process, but the result of a dance may be something else entirely. The first impulse that a choreographer has can change significantly through the choreographic process until the dance no longer resembles the original idea. If you are looking for the idea behind the dance, it may not be easy to find, since the idea could have morphed into something less distinct from the beginning concept.

Even if the idea of the dance has remained the same during its creation, or the new idea is a very clear one, the choreographer's intention is only one piece of information about a dance. The choreographer may not even be aware of many of the images that appear in the final dance. Your experience in the world will allow you to see different images in the dance. Take a dance in which a dancer turns away dramatically from her reflection in a mirror. Perhaps the choreographer's inspiration for creating this movement was an unpleasant experience with body image. As a viewer, you may not have any experience with body image issues. In this case you interpret this movement as an expression of guilt. Both of these interpretations of the movement are valid. Simply because the movement was created by the chore-ographer to mean one thing doesn't mean it can't mean something else to you. The more abstract the images in the dance, the more likely you are to have your own interpretation of the dance based on your own experiences. This is encouraged! Let the dance speak to you.

Quality and Mood

Your analysis of a dance tells the reader not only what the dancers did but also how they did it. Perhaps the dancers jump frequently. This could give the impression of joy, or it could portray fear and apprehension. In the analysis of the dance, you would include an explanation of the qualities of the movement and the mood that the piece embodies to you based on your observations of these movement qualities.

Image Identification

Descriptions of mood are not effective if they are not backed up with a description of an image. Examples of ineffective descriptions are "When the woman was lifted by the man, she appeared to fly above the crowd of dancers," or maybe "When the woman was lifted, she appeared to be isolated on top of a mountain." Just describ-ing this as a lift deprives the reader of the rich artistic imagery that a dance can contain. Finding the images in a work that are the most memorable to you is key to understanding what a dance is about. Saying that the dance appeared to be about depression is validated by a description of the image of how isolated dancers moved low in tense, slow phrases. Image identification is the process of putting together movement descriptions so that they create meaningful moments in the dance for the reader.

Searching for Metaphor

One way to analyze your observations about a dance is to look for the metaphor of the dance. A metaphor, in this sense, is an imaginative reality that is created by the dance. You know that the experience on stage is not real, yet it relates to real life. Maybe abstract moving formations in a dance remind you of the way particles move under a microscope or reflect the patterns of the stars at night. Even if there is no character or obvious setting in a dance, the metaphor created by the choreographer can be a point of discussion with others or the subject of your writing. Asking yourself to find the metaphor of a dance is a way of analyzing all of the elements in a dance and looking at their cumulative effect on you as a viewer. This is the point in your paper where you explain how the images you identified in the dance come together to create meaning.

Evaluation

Once you have described the dance, including the imagery you see in the work and the metaphor or imaginative reality that the piece communicates, then you are ready to evaluate the effectiveness of the piece. The evaluation could be related to how well the dance's metaphor reads to you as an audience member, how coherent a work seems as a means of communication, or whether the elements of the piece come together in a cohesive way. Sometimes an evaluation of a dance includes critical commentary on the technique of the performers or some other specific element of a performance. Your instructor may give you things to look for in a performance, such as the use of music or the specific style of movements that the dancers perform. It is appropriate to comment on these elements in the evaluation section of your paper as well. Some professional dance critics compare the dances they see with the reputation or history of that dance company or some other external standards. Check with your teacher to determine whether there are certain criteria that he would like you to respond to when you write about dance.

Be patient with yourself. Writing about dance is a rewarding activity, but like any other process, it takes practice. The more you write and share your experiences in viewing dance live and on video, the more you will get out of it. You need to consider and review many factors when you describe a dance, but learning to pay attention to these elements not only will help you to describe what you see but will lead you to seeing more in the dances you view. Many of the skills you use in learning movement carry over to viewing dances and vice versa. Learning to be a close observer in the studio will benefit you when you see dance in the theater, and consequently seeing dance in the theater and reflecting on it critically will help you be an observant student in the studio.

SUMMARY

As part of studying modern dance, you will learn to remember dance sequences for performance. In addition to practicing, several strategies can enhance your memory. Note taking is a particularly important part of developing your memory skills, especially when you learn to focus on the what, where, when, with whom, how, and why of the choreography. Another important part of understanding the art form of modern dance is to see live and videotaped professional performances. Learning to notice and describe how choreographers use certain elements to get ideas across will aid you in describing and reflecting on what you see. The most important elements to explain are the names and numbers of the artists; the music used for the dance; the movement vocabulary, structure, and sequence of the dance; and how all of these combine to create mood and images. Reflection on all of these elements will help you to find a metaphor that unites the dance into a cohesive idea communicated by the choreographer, which you will describe, analyze, and evaluate. The more you learn to describe dance you see in a performance, the better you will be at understanding dance in the studio.

To find supplementary materials for this chapter, such as learning activities, e-journal assignments, and web links, visit the web resource at **www.HumanKinetics.com/BeginningModernDance1E.**

Chapter 7

History of Modern Dance

A wonderful thing about dance is that not only can you connect to it physically in the studio, but you can connect to it emotionally and intellectually as well. The more you know about the history and philosophy of modern dancers, the more you can appreciate how this art form integrates mind and body and how it has changed over time to be the type of dance you are studying today.

This chapter looks at the events in history that led to the birth of modern dance in the late 19th and early 20th centuries. It also covers the dancers and choreographers who pioneered this art form and examines how they saw the body as a tool of expression or design in space. Like all artists, these figures in modern dance history were influenced by the society in which they lived. Three major developments in society influenced the development of modern dance: the women's movement, industrialism, and an era of social and political change.

ORIGINS OF MODERN DANCE

The art form of modern dance was born in the latter years of the 19th century and developed into a new form of dance in the early years of the 20th century. To understand how a new art form arose, you must look at the times in which it was created.

The Women's Movement

Many factors led to the emergence of the women's movement in Europe and the United States in the late 19th century. Women were working more outside the home as factories replaced home-based industries. Although women were entering the industrial work force, an attitude of inequality prevailed. Basic rights such as equal pay for women and the right to vote were denied.

These struggles to be considered equal to and independent from men under the law did not always connect with the depictions of women in classical dance in the 19th century, which frequently featured fantasy stories of a prince rescuing a damsel in distress. Some women began to wonder whether there might be another way to express themselves through movement that did not perpetuate the image of a woman as dependent on a man to rescue her. The early pioneers of modern dance sought to replace this image of the innocent ingénue with a woman of independent spirit who moved her body with force.

Industrialization

The late 19th century was a time of mechanization. New inventions were springing up that were changing the way of life. The electric light bulb, telephone, and sewing machine were all invented between 1870 and 1880. Everyone seemed fascinated with the modern, "scientific" way of doing things. Dance was no exception. Two men were particularly prominent in popularizing an analytical approach to looking at movement at the end of the 19th and beginning of the 20th centuries. These two men were François Delsarte and Rudolf von Laban.

François Delsarte

François Delsarte (1811-1871) was a French music teacher who developed a system to help performers enhance their bodily expressiveness. Delsarte used this analysis to teach dramatic gestures to his pupils, which he believed led to the development of aesthetic principles, many of which were related to the look of ancient Greek artwork like bas reliefs or painted vases. Delsarte's approach captured the imagination of many women in the United States who practiced his methods regularly in what was often referred to as Delsartean exercise.

> **DID YOU KNOW?** ▶ ▷ ▷ ▷ ▷ ▷ ▷
>
> If you have seen the movie version of *The Music Man*, then you have seen Delsartean exercise! The mayor's wife, Eulalie Shinn, leads a group of women in posing like Grecian urns. This is an approximation, although exaggerated and humorous, of the practice of Delsartean exercise.

He believed that movement achieved its greatest effect with the least amount of effort. He was even quoted as saying that grace was the efficiency of movement. It is no wonder his work was so well received in a time fascinated with scientific advancement through mechanical efficiency.

Rudolf von Laban

Rudolf von Laban (1879-1958) was a Hungarian-born teacher and ballet director who analyzed what he considered to be the laws of dynamics and expression in human movement. This analytical approach to how humans move later led to Laban movement analysis, a system for analyzing the specific ways in which the body can move, and Labanotation, a symbol system for recording any kind of human movement, especially choreography. More details regarding the principles on which Laban based his work are in chapter 4. His precise approach to decoding the way humans move and express themselves was a fashionable concept in the early 20th century. It played into the popularity of the new and scientific approaches to bettering daily lives. As a teacher, Laban was an influence on both Mary Wigman and Kurt Jooss, the two most memorable choreographers of early modern dance in Germany.

New Trends in Visual Art

No art form stands alone. In the beginning of the 20th century, there were new trends in visual art that influenced the early modern dancers and choreographers.

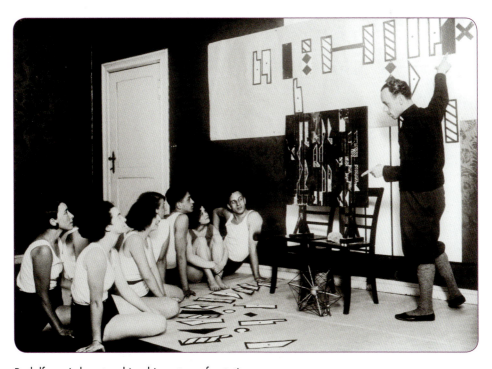

Rudolf von Laban teaching his system of notation.

Visual artists of this time were reciprocally influenced by the modern dance style that was just beginning.

Art Nouveau

One popular trend in art in the late 19th and early 20th centuries was the art nouveau movement. This style of art and architecture took its inspiration from aspects of nature. Poster artists and painters of the day such as Alphonse Mucha, Jules Chéret, and Henri de Toulouse-Lautrec were particularly fond of using images of the "new woman," who rejected conventional views of domesticity and femininity. Not surprisingly, many of the early modern dance pioneers were the subjects of this poster art.

> ## DID YOU KNOW? ▶▶▶ ▶ ▶ ▶ ▶ ▶
>
> Modern dance got its name not only because it was a new and modern form of dance at the beginning of the 20th century but also because of its similarity to modernism in art.

Modernism Versus Realism

Many artists engaged in a deliberate departure from realistic depiction in art to what became known as modernism. This new style explored subjective experience, such as one's feelings and perceptions, rather than observed real life. The work looked abstract as opposed to realistic. The works of painter Pablo Picasso, which contain recognizable body parts but not the realistic face of a woman, are an example of this modernist movement in art. The new dance, or modern dance as it later became known, was interested in depicting the abstraction of human experience rather than a realistic retelling of a story. The new dance explored personal feelings about the world through abstracted, uncluttered, nonliteral movement, just as modern art depicted the artist's subjective views of the world through abstracted shapes and often more simplified compositions. Like modernism in art, modern dance manifested itself as a rebellion against the artistic traditions of the past.

A Century of Social and Political Change

Every artist is a product of the time in which he or she creates. While early modern dance artists were frequently on the cutting edge of change, many also reflected the prejudices and circumstances of their times.

The search for the elements of dance was a driving force for many artists in the beginning of the 20th century. This exploration led many choreographers to an interest in Native American and African American dance and music because of a perception that these forms are based on primitive, elemental rhythms and movements. While many of the early modern artists, such as Helen Tamiris in her signature work *Negro Spirituals* (1928), took up the theme of diversity, these dances did not cast African Americans as the performers. Similarly, Martha Graham's *American Document* (1938) showcased episodes of Native American and African American history but did not include any members of these groups in the cast. This and other similar examples reflect the racial segregation prevalent in American society before 1960.

Political views and causes, in particular fighting fascism, found their way into the artistic revolt that was modern dance. Artists such as Anna Sokolow, Helen Tamiris, and Sophie Maslow responded through dance to issues of class struggle and the need for social change in America. Modern dancers in general were concerned with the tension between individual expression and the possibilities of the new art form to express wider societal issues.

EVOLUTION OF MODERN DANCE

Masterworks are dances that either transcend the time in which they were created so they stay relevant or so clearly represent the time in which they were made that they survive. While it isn't possible to give adequate recognition to all of the choreographers, producers, educators, and dancers who shaped modern dance, several prominent individuals and masterworks can help in tracing the development of the art form as it is practiced in the studio and often performed today. This brief history of modern dance divides the years of the 20th century into five time periods and a descriptive word or phrase, which typifies the artists of that period.

1900-1920: Matriarchs

The story of modern dance, or "new dance" as it was called at the time, begins with three women who are often seen as the mothers of the art form and the foundation of the modern dance family tree. These women are Loie Fuller, Isadora Duncan, and Ruth St. Denis. Each made a unique contribution to the development of the genre. Table 7.1 is a timeline of historical and modern dance events from 1900 to 1919.

Loie Fuller

Loie Fuller (1862-1928) was born Marie Louise Fuller in Illinois. Her choreography was an event of total theater. She took huge pieces of fabric draped on her arms and body, sometimes augmented by sticks in the sleeves, and manipulated them under lights to create magnificent effects. Her dances were mainly solo works for herself, where she was transformed on stage into the heart of a fire or the serpentine shapes of a butterfly's wings. Fuller's show was a spectacle. Today's rock concerts in their extravagant use of lighting and sets were probably the equivalent experience for Fuller's audiences in the late 1800s and early 1900s.

Fuller made two contributions to the emergent art form of modern dance. She was the first choreographer to insist on a completely darkened theater for her performances, something taken for granted in theater performances today. She demanded this in part because her work depended on lighting effects, the second of her remarkable innovations. Loie Fuller, along with her team of electricians,

Table 7.1 Significant Events From 1900 to 1919

1900	Sigmund Freud publishes *Interpretation of Dreams*. Loie Fuller performs in the Paris Exposition
1902	Duncan performs in Budapest in a sold out run for 30 days.
1902	Loie Fuller meets Isadora Duncan.
1903	Wright Brothers' first flight.
1905	St. Denis performs *Radha*.
1906	Six-year-old Fred Astaire does his first performance with his sister Adele.
1907	Anna Pavlova performs the "Dying Swan" solo.
1908	First radio transmissions. Ford Motor Company invents the assembly line.
1910	Ruth St. Denis performs *Egypta*.
1912	*Titanic* sinks.
1913	Niels Bohr creates first model of atomic nucleus. Isadora Duncan's image sculpted in the walls of the Théâtre des Champs-Élysées.
1914	Ruth St. Denis and Ted Shawn form the Denishawn School.
1916	Einstein's theory of general relativity published. Duncan tours extensively in Europe and United States through 1920.
1917	Russian Revolution.
1918	End of World War I. Women's suffrage is achieved in UK.

designed and implemented the first system of projected stage light, including calcium and incandescent light, revolving dishes, and lighting gels to change the color of the light.

Fuller was on the cutting edge of the technology of her time. Her work with light and fabric reflected the interest in all things technological at the turn of the century. The flowing shapes created by the fabrics and light she manipulated mirrored the natural, organic forms of the art nouveau movement—and she was a complete departure from the narrative-driven dances of the time. Fuller's work did not need plot or characters; it relied instead on imagery abstracted from the natural world, the first of the dance artists to connect with this modernist trend.

Fuller was also the first of the era of new dance to train dancers in her style and the first dancer to shed her corset in performance. To many, appearing in public without a corset was scandalous and improper. To the new woman at the beginning of the women's movement, however, it symbolized freedom from the containment of women's limited roles in society. Fuller was an iconic image for this new woman. There is some evidence from their writings that both Isadora Duncan and Ruth St. Denis were two such new women who saw Loie Fuller perform and were impressed and inspired by her work.

Loie Fuller in her butterfly dress, 1901.

Isadora Duncan

Isadora Duncan (1877-1927) was born in California. In her brief lifetime, she made some of the most significant contributions to the development of modern dance. Duncan's dances were based on simple movements, such as walking or skipping, and dramatic gestures. She practiced what she called music visualization, where she listened to music and brought the feeling and emotion contained in it to life through her body. Duncan felt that dance was the embodiment of emotion, and her dances dealt with fundamental feelings such as joy, anger, and fear. Duncan said that motion is motivated by emotion and must be expressed with the instrument of the entire human body (Duncan 1928). Isadora was inspired by the art of ancient Greece and the work of François Delsarte, so it is not surprising that poses reminiscent of sculptures or figures on Greek bas reliefs made their way into her aesthetic. Many of these poses were natural, rather than formal, and seldom used turned-out legs.

DID YOU KNOW? ▶ ▶ ▶ ▶ ▶ ▶ ▶ ▶

One piece of artwork of which Duncan was particularly fond was Botticelli's famous painting *Primavera*. This work portrays Greek women in flowing, diaphanous robes celebrating the spring. Isadora's costuming frequently mirrored those in this painting.

One of Duncan's most significant contributions to the new dance (not yet coined *modern*) was her obvious and intentional use of breath. Having removed her corset, Isadora is reputed to have spent time in the studio watching the rise and fall of her breath in the mirror. She studied its effect on her movement and the ways in which her torso could move in response. The use of breath as a motivation for movement, or the consideration of breath patterns in a piece of choreography, is central to the practice of modern dance today. Isadora Duncan laid this foundation in the very early years of the 20th century.

Isadora Duncan dancing in the waves.

Ruth St. Denis

Ruth St. Denis (1879-1968) was born in New Jersey. As a child, St. Denis, actually named Ruth Dennis, studied Delsartean exercise, ballet, and some social dance forms. She moved to New York to dance in vaudeville in 1892. There she was discovered by the legendary Broadway producer and director David Belasco, who hired her to be a featured dancer in his touring production of Zaza. St. Denis, as Belasco had renamed her, toured for several years with the great actress Sarah Bernhardt, whose physically dramatic acting style was influential on the young dancer. In 1904 St. Denis saw an advertisement for Egyptian Deities cigarettes, featuring the goddess Isis. Miss Ruth, as she would later be called, already an avid reader of history and ancient cultures, became fascinated with ancient Egypt and India. Inspired by the Orient, as the East was known at the time, St. Denis began a solo career with the creation of the dance *Radha*, which was St. Denis' embodiment of her understanding of Indian culture and mythology.

Ruth St. Denis brought new dance forward in two significant ways. The dances she created were researched interpretations of other cultures that brought new steps into the vocabulary of dance. The development of new movements and the discovery of new ways to move the body are an ongoing part of the art form of modern dance, a tradition tracing back to Ruth St. Denis. Her second major contribution to the art form was popularizing the new dance by bringing it to much larger numbers of viewers through vaudeville. This is an adventure she cocreated with Ted Shawn, whom you will learn about in the next section.

1920-1940: Pioneers

In the 1920s new dance became more solidified, and it established itself as an art form in its own right. By the early 1930s it took on the name *modern dance*. Choreographers and dancers began identifying as modern dance artists and began writing in defense of its existence as a genre of dance. Specific styles began to emerge in this period as various dancers and choreographers developed differing philosophies of how the body communicates through dance (see table 7.2).

Ted Shawn and Ruth St. Denis, in many ways, are the figures that link the two generations of dancers, the matriarchs and the pioneers. They are the bridge between the generation that invented a new way of moving and the generation that

Table 7.2   Significant Events From 1920 to 1939

1920	Women get the right to vote in the United States.
	Mary Wigman opens her school in Berlin.
1923	Charleston dance craze.
1924	Gershwin composes *Rhapsody in Blue*.
1925	Scopes Monkey Trial supporting the right to teach the theory of evolution in schools.
1926	Martha Graham holds first concert of her own work.
1927	*The Jazz Singer*, first talking movie, opens.
	Lindbergh's first solo flight across the Atlantic.
	Ted Shawn performs at Carnegie Hall.
1928	Alexander Fleming discovers penicillin.
	Mickey Mouse is created.
	Doris Humphrey leaves Denishawn.
1929	Wall Street crash begins the Great Depression.
1930	Mary Wigman tours the United States.
1931	"Star Spangled Banner" adopted as the U.S. national anthem.
	Ted Shawn buys Jacob's Pillow Farm and begins a dance retreat there.
	Doris Humphrey choreographs *The Shakers*.
1935	Martha Graham choreographs *Frontier* with a set by Isamu Noguchi.
1936	Katherine Dunham goes to Haiti to study Caribbean dance rituals
1937	Beginning of World War II.
	Snow White animated movie premiers.
1938	First appearance of *Superman* comic.
1939	RCA pavilion at the World's Fair introduces television to the United States.

modulated that new way into an art form. In their lengthy careers, they oversaw the transition from scattered artists in the new dance into the movement that became known as modern dance.

Ted Shawn

Ted Shawn (1891-1972) was born in Missouri. As with many men encountered in the story of modern dance, Shawn did not set out to be a dancer; in fact, he began his college career as a divinity student at the University of Denver. In 1911 he saw Ruth St. Denis perform on tour and was moved by her work. In 1914 he went to New York to study with her and they became partners both on and off the stage. They married in 1914, although the "new woman" St. Denis refused to say the word *obey* in their wedding ceremony.

For the next several years, Shawn and St. Denis made three powerful contributions to the growth of the art form known today as modern dance. The first was through their extensive touring. Together Shawn and St. Denis created huge pageantlike shows that toured through the vaudeville circuit, booking 56 weeks of engagements in 1915 and 1916. From 1921 to 1925 they were the highest-paid dance company in the United States. This meant that larger numbers of people were being exposed to this new art form. The familiarity of St. Denis and Shawn helped to put new dance ideas in front of the general public and gain their acceptance.

Ruth St. Denis and Ted Shawn's second major contribution to the development of the genre was the creation of the first school of modern dance in the United States. It was called Denishawn, a compilation of both the founders' names. Founded in 1915 they taught an eclectic selection of dance styles, including music visualization, Delsartean exercise, "Oriental" dance for spirituality, ballet technique, yoga, meditation, and free movement (what might be termed improvisation). One of the

Ruth St. Denis and Denishawn dancers in yoga meditation, 1915.

most important aspects of the school was the students. Doris Humphrey, Martha Graham, and Charles Weidman, who all figure prominently in the growth of modern dance, met and were trained at Denishawn.

Ted Shawn's contributions as the first prominent male dancer and his advocacy of the male role in the new art form have earned him the title of father of modern dance. Years after his work at Denishawn, in fact, Shawn formed an all-male company called Ted Shawn and His Dancers, who toured widely, spreading the idea that the new idiom of modern dance was not only for women. It was also Papa Shawn who demanded that newspapers pay attention to modern dance and was in part responsible for the advent of professional dance critics in newspapers. Shawn is probably best remembered, however, for creating the Jacob's Pillow dance retreat, which is still in operation today, as a destination for cutting-edge modern dance.

Doris Humphrey

Doris Humphrey (1895-1958) was born in Illinois. After an early dance career as a dance teacher in the Midwest, Humphrey traveled to Denishawn in 1917. She spent 10 years studying and performing with Ruth St. Denis and Ted Shawn. She received her early choreographic

> ### DID YOU KNOW? ▶▶▶▶▶▶▶
> Doris Humphrey was often challenged to define and defend this new form of concert dance. In response, she wrote *The Art of Making Dances*, which articulated the principles on which her choreography was based.

experiences there as well, even collaborating with Miss Ruth on two enduring works, *Soaring* (1920) and *Sonata Pathetique* (1920). She, alongside fellow Denishawn student Charles Weidman, however, became somewhat disenchanted with Denishawn. Humphrey also wanted to dance about her American heritage, not the East, and believed the nascent art form of modern dance should be developing in the direction of abstraction and true modernism. Humphrey felt the dances of Denishawn were sentimental and romantic, not reflective of the modern lifestyle of the 20th century.

Leaving Denishawn in 1928 with Charles Weidman, Humphrey began an illustrious career as a choreographer. She focused on group choreography rather than the solo style, which had been popular at the time, and claimed that group dances showed the fullest potential of the medium. Several of her dances had American themes. Her work *The Shakers* (1931), for example, explored the world of that American ecstatic religious sect, and her dance *Day on Earth* (1941) commented on the life of the modern family.

One of the key principles of Humphrey's work is that movement is an activity that occurs between falling and recovering, between balance and the loss of balance, between the in breath and the out breath. According to Humphrey, patterns of group movement consist of unison (doing the same thing at the same time), succession (doing the same thing but at different times, as in a canon or round in music), and opposition (doing different things at the same time). These terms still represent key ideas in modern dance and choreographic process today. You will learn much more about Doris Humphrey in chapter 8, since her technique survives today as the Humphrey-Limón technique.

Martha Graham

Martha Graham (1894-1991), the most well-known modern dancer of the 20th century, was born in Pennsylvania. Like Humphrey, Graham had been a student at Denishawn who quickly rose to a central role as both dancer and teacher at the school. She, too, left Denishawn to pursue her own career. In 1927, Graham began to establish herself as a performer in New York. Her work was based on the Delsartean principle of tension and relaxation, which she adapted and developed into the concept of contraction and release. (A contraction is the tensing of a muscle; a release is the energy that results from relaxing that same muscle.) Emphasis on these movements often gave Graham's work a sharp and angular appearance, resonant with many art forms of the 1930s. Some of Graham's earlier work, such as the iconic solo *Lamentation* (1930), in which Graham danced the idea of grief while wrapped in a large swath of fabric, reminded critics of the modern architecture in New York City.

Like Humphrey, Graham wanted to make dances that reflected the American experience. Many of her earlier works, such as *Primitive Mysteries* (1931), a dance about Native American religious rituals, and *Appalachian Spring* (1944), about a wedding in the Appalachian Mountains, showed idealized pictures of American life. The latter dance includes a sparse abstracted house on stage created by Isamu Noguchi, the modern sculptor, who created sets for many of Graham's most famous dances. Graham's close connection to the modern art and architecture of the 1930s and 1940s was another step in establishing the validity of modern dance as a serious art form and another way in which modern dance and modernism are linked.

While Graham's work from the 1930s and 1940s was marked by a distinctly American focus, her later work took on another quality. After her divorce from fellow dancer Erick Hawkins, Graham began to explore the darker side of human nature. Many of her later works, such as *Night Journey* (1947) and *Clytemnestra* (1958), were based in Greek mythology, probably due to her interest in Jungian psychology. Many more were introspective and psychological. Many of Martha Graham's dances have survived to today, as has her dance company, which is based in New York. Much more information about the principles of the Graham technique appears in chapter 8.

Graham, like her contemporary Doris Humphrey, advanced the changing status of women in society. The very fact that these women held prominent jobs as choreographers, teachers, and directors made it clear that women could take a central role in the building and shaping of American culture.

Mary Wigman

Mary Wigman (1886-1973) was born in Hanover, Germany. Considered the pioneer of modern dance in Germany, Wigman was a prominent student of Rudolf von Laban. As a performer, Wigman's emotionally laden pieces were characterized by kneeling and crouching and a strong sense of gravity. Much of her choreography did not use music or used only percussion. One of Wigman's greatest contributions to modern dance was as a teacher. Wigman opened a school of modern dance in Germany in 1920 and, as with the Denishawn school, many future innovators came to study there. Wigman's principles of movement were based on rhythm and emotion. She developed dance phrases from body rhythms and was interested in presenting emotional experience through movement. Wigman's ideas made their way to the United States through her pupil Hanya Holm.

Katherine Dunham

Katherine Dunham (1909-2006) was born in Illinois. As a teenager, she studied ballet in Chicago with Ruth Page and danced with Ballet Negre, one of the first African American ballet companies. Since the beginning of her college career at the University of Chicago, where she discovered a passion for anthropology, Dunham sought to synthesize her love of both academics and dance. As part of her education, Dunham traveled to Haiti in the 1930s to study Haitian dance rituals. On her return from Haiti, Dunham created a series of dance performances based on the culture and practices of the Caribbean. The authenticity of her choreography brought a real taste of Afro-Caribbean culture into the public eye and into the world of modern dance. Her company, the Katherine Dunham Dance Company, based in New York, toured the world for over two decades. Dunham choreographed not only for her company but also for Broadway and film, and she has the distinction of being the first African American choreographer for the Metropolitan Opera. Dunham was an influential teacher, opening schools in both New York and East St. Louis, where she trained generations of dancers, including some of the most memorable of the next generation of modern dance, such as Talley Beatty and Alvin Ailey. Dunham codified her technique, which is a synthesis of Western, African, and Caribbean forms. Students at the Dunham School can become certified teachers in her technique, which grew and evolved throughout Dunham's 70-year career as a dancer, teacher, and choreographer. Dunham was a pioneer of African American modern dance, bringing the voice of the African diaspora into the development of the art form of modern dance. While African American concert dancers rejoiced in their anthropological roots in African and the Caribbean, it may have been in part because they were unable to find sufficient support as part of the predominantly white modern dance community. Dunham's influence, however, reverberates throughout the field of concert dance for dancers of all ethnicities.

1940-1960: Second Generation, the Legacy Builders

By the 1940s, modern dance had established itself as an accepted form of concert dance. Dancers were training in the various styles that had developed during the pioneers' generation (see table 7.3). Two prominent performers and teachers have helped to keep the art form of modern dance alive as the pioneers designed it. These were José Limón and Hanya Holm.

Table 7.3   Significant Events From 1940 to 1959

1940	McDonald's is founded.
1941	Attack on Pearl Harbor. Katherine Dunham choreographs *Rites de Passage*.
1945	End of World War II, creation of the atomic bomb. Lester Horton choreographs *Salome*.
1946	ENIAC, first general-purpose computer, is invented. First bikini is designed.
1947	José Limón forms José Limón Dance Company.
1948	Alwin Nikolais is appointed director of the Henry Street Playhouse. Lester Horton choreographs *The Beloved*. Hanya Holm choreographs *Kiss Me Kate* on Broadway. Hanya Holm's Labanotation for *Kiss Me Kate* becomes the first copyrighted dance in America.
1949	José Limón choreographs *The Moor's Pavane*.
1950	Beginning of Korean War. First credit card is introduced.
1953	Watson and Crick discover the structure of DNA. Merce Cunningham choreographs *Suite by Chance*. Merce Cunningham forms Merce Cunningham Dance Company.
1954	*Brown v. Board of Education* ends racial segregation in U.S. schools.
1955	Jonas Salk develops vaccine for polio.
1956	Nikolais Dance Theater's first performance at the American Dance Festival.
1957	Launch of *Sputnik I* and beginning of space age. *American Bandstand* premieres.
1958	Peace sign is first used. NASA is founded.
1959	Beginning of Vietnam War. Incorporation of Alaska and Hawaii as U.S. states. Barbie doll is introduced.

José Limón

José Limón (1908-1972) was born in Mexico, although he moved to Arizona in 1915 and lived the rest of his life in the United States. Limón studied painting until the age of 20, when he saw his first dance concert and enrolled to study with Doris Humphrey in 1929. This was the beginning of a 30-year creative collaboration between the two artists. Limón danced many roles for the Humphrey-Weidman

Company, and in one *New York Times* article he was hailed as the finest male dancer of his time. He began his own company in 1947, with Doris Humphrey as its resident choreographer. Many of Limón's dances, particularly *The Moor's Pavane* (1949), an abstract retelling of Shakespeare's Othello, are in the repertory of major ballet companies around the world. The Limón Company, based in New York, still performs and tours internationally.

Limón further codified and developed the technique of his teacher Doris Humphrey, but he did not consider his developments to be a new style; rather, it was an embellishment of the Humphrey tradition. This is why the technique is known as the Humphrey- Limón technique today. Limón's prominence as a choreographer and performer helped to keep the technique in the forefront of dance education where it is still embraced today. Much more is covered about this technique in chapter 8.

Hanya Holm

Hanya Holm (1893-1992) was born in Germany. Holm began studying with Mary Wigman in 1921. A talented dancer, Holm eventually became the chief instructor and codirector of the Wigman School in Dresden, Germany. By 1931, when Wigman had decided to start a branch of her school in the United States, it was Hanya Holm who was sent to create and direct the American Wigman School. Holm's work was closely related to that of Laban and Wigman. She used their principles to explore space and believed that the body should be used as a tool to express emotion. Her views on teaching, however, put her at odds with Mary Wigman. Holm wanted to modify the technique to suit the American women who were studying there. Mary Wigman, caught up in the pre–World War II politics of Germany, including her sympathy for the Nazi movement, was uncomfortable with Holm's modifications and with the presence of Jewish dancers who attended the classes. She removed her name from the school and it became known as the Hanya Holm School of Dance in 1936. Holm, a brilliant educator, saw technique class as a way of training the body without teaching stylization. This approach was popular with modern dance teachers of the 1940s and 1950s because it was so adaptable. Its popularity ensured that the Wigman and Laban principles were passed to the next generation of modern dancers.

1940-1960: Second Generation, the Iconoclasts

At the same time that pupils of pioneers like Holm and Limón were keeping the classical modern dance of the pioneers alive, new artists were working to change what the art form had become. Modern dance began out of rebellion, and it was following that tradition. The only difference was that now, modern dance was an established-enough institution to rebel against!

While the love of nature and art nouveau was no longer in vogue, modernism was still a driving force in the art world. World War II—especially its ending with the dropping of the atomic bomb—changed the world, and the arts responded. Civil rights had joined women's rights as a cause célèbre, and these issues brought about the development of the art form. The first computers were being developed and, by the end of that generation, were finding their way into choreography.

Modern dance was still responding to the changes and social trends of the day. This is demonstrated through the work of three iconoclastic choreographers. An **iconoclast** is a person who challenges tradition, and that term describes the three artists who were part of the next generation of modern dance.

Merce Cunningham

Merce Cunningham (1919-2009) was born in Washington State. As a young dancer, Cunningham studied a variety of techniques, including ballet, folk, tap, ballroom, and Graham-style modern dance. Cunningham, in fact, danced with the Graham Company from 1940 to 1945, when he began his own company, the Merce Cunningham Dance Company. The company remained in existence until his death in 2009. Cunningham's work will live on, however, through a legacy project, which preserves work and makes it available for reconstruction through electronic resources. It should come as no surprise that Cunningham's legacy is innovative and technological. These were the hallmarks of his entire career.

Cunningham's dances, especially those beginning in the 1950s, incorporated the element of random chance. In *Suite by Chance* (1953), a coin toss backstage determined several elements of the piece before each performance. In *Dime a Dance* (1953), the audience drew cards to determine the order of sections of the dance. These dances, created within five years of the dropping of the atomic bomb, reflected the general sense in the world that anything could happen at any time. This was also the era of the first computers, which had the ability to generate random numbers electronically. A sense of the randomness of events was on many people's minds, and it came through in Cunningham's dances. The music, too, included elements of the unpredictable. Many of Cunningham's dances were accompanied by scores created by modern composer John Cage. These nonmetric soundscapes were created through the use of computers or other electronic equipment. The dancers in the pieces rehearsed in silence and would hear the music for the first time in performance. Cunningham revolutionized the world of dance by saying that the only connection between music and dance was that they were occupying the theater at the same time.

Cunningham believed that the element of random chance and the separation of music and dance led to freedom in choreography. He did not believe that emotion was the motivation for dancing. He believed that the subject of dancing was dance itself and that movement should be regarded as moving design, not a visualization of the music or the exposition of an emotional state. Much more is said about the Cunningham technique in chapter 8.

Cunningham's dances were also marked by a strong connection to visual art, including in later years the art of media, animation, and technology. The most well-known pop artists of the 1950s and 1960s, including Andy Warhol, Robert Rauschenberg, and Jasper Johns, were frequent collaborators in the design of Cunningham's work. The cerebral, conceptual nature of modern art mirrored the nonemotional, abstracted, design-driven dances that Cunningham created.

Cunningham typified the next generation of iconoclasts who focused on deepening abstraction.

Lester Horton

Lester Horton (1906-1953) was born in Indiana. His early experiences as a dancer were broad and eclectic. He had experiences with Native American culture, musical theater, nightclubs, and concert dance. He brought all of these ideas and experiences into his choreography for the Horton Dance Theater and School, which was formed in 1942. Horton's work was largely narrative and theatrical, often with political overtones. His most widely known dance, *The Beloved* (1948), tells the story of an adulterous woman killed by her preacher husband.

The work itself was not his only political connection to the times. In the late 1930s and early 1940s, many schools of dance refused to enroll non-White students. Horton, a proponent of the civil rights movement, allowed any dancer to take class. In fact, his was the first fully integrated dance company, including African American, Japanese, and Caucasian dancers. Many of his company members went on to create companies of their own, the most famous of whom was Alvin Ailey.

Horton was also an outstanding educator and, together with Bella Lewitzky, developed what is still known as the Horton technique. Many well-known second-generation Horton students, such as James Truitte and Joyce Trisler, have disseminated his technique all over the world, and it is still popular today. Much more information about the Horton technique is in chapter 8.

Lester Horton teaching a class on choreography.

Alwin Nikolais

Alwin Nikolais (1910-1993) was born in Connecticut. As a young man he played piano to accompany silent films, but then he saw a dance concert given by Mary Wigman and decided to change his path to study dance. He became a student of many of the pioneers, including Hanya Holm, Martha Graham, Charles Weidman, and Louis Horst. In 1948, after several years as Hanya Holm's assistant, Nikolais was appointed director of the Henry Street Playhouse in New York. It is there that he made his most significant contributions to the art of modern dance.

Nikolais began creating dances of abstract total theater. Nikolais not only choreographed the dances, but he composed the sound scores and designed the sets, props, and costumes for his dances as well. He believed that dancers were not specific individuals with theatrical characterizations, but they were people in the environment of the stage. He is quoted as saying that dance is the art of motion, not emotion. Nikolais dances took the abstraction of the body to new extremes. Dancers were frequently covered entirely in large pieces of fabric, as in *Noumenon Mobilus* (1953), or they wore sculptural extensions to their limbs, as in *Imago Suite* (1963), so that the body became a moving set piece. His work is a true departure from the early pioneers, who saw the body as a tool of emotional expression. The bodies in a work by Alwin Nikolais are moving parts within an imaginary landscape. Created in the age of computers and electronically synthesized music, Nikolais' work reflects the connection of man and his manufactured environment.

Alwin Nikolais.

1960-1980: Synthesizers

The next generation of modern dance would also reflect the diverse and chaotic times in which it was created. The 1960s and 1970s were a time of sweeping changes in civil rights legislation in the United States, rapid growth in computer technology, and the beginning of globalization (see table 7.4). African American dance was embraced by the mainstream of the art form, and choreographers were beginning to fuse together elements of the many distinct styles of modern dance that had emerged in the previous generations. In fact, modern dance was becoming

Table 7.4   Significant Events From 1960 to 1979

1960	The Beatles form in Liverpool. Alvin Ailey choreographs *Revelations*.
1961	Peace Corps is founded.
1962	Cuban Missile Crisis. Paul Taylor choreographs *Aureole*.
1963	Martin Luther King Jr. delivers his *I Have a Dream* speech. Assassination of President John F. Kennedy.
1964	U.S. civil rights act is passed. Miniskirt is created by Mary Quant in London.
1965	Twyla Tharp choreographs *Tank Dive*.
1967	First heart transplant is performed.
1968	Assassination of Martin Luther King Jr. First Special Olympics.
1969	Moon landing. Woodstock music festival. Alvin Ailey American Dance Theatre becomes company in residence at Brooklyn Academy of Music.
1971	Alvin Ailey choreographs *Cry* solo for Judith Jamison.
1973	Watergate scandal.
1974	President Richard Nixon resigns. Bar code is invented.
1975	End of Vietnam War. Paul Taylor choreographs *Esplanade*.
1976	Twyla Tharp choreographs *Push Comes to Shove*.
1977	First mass-produced personal computers, including Apple II. *Star Wars* premiers.
1979	Sony Walkman is introduced.

known as the genre of dance characterized by change. The following three masters of the genre typify these changes.

Alvin Ailey

Alvin Ailey (1931-1989) was born in Texas. As a young man, Ailey studied under Hanya Holm, Martha Graham, and Charles Weidman. He studied dance composition, or choreography class, with Doris Humphrey. His real contribution to the art form came when he joined Lester Horton's company in 1950. A leader from the beginning, Ailey was appointed director of the Horton Company just three years later upon Horton's death in 1953. After five years of directing Horton's company on the West Coast, Ailey moved east to begin his own dance company, the Alvin Ailey American Dance Theatre (AAADT), in 1958. A remarkable and prolific choreographer, Ailey created masterwork dances, such as his signature *Revelations* (1960), which are iconic of African American concert dance. The company was a representative of the civil rights era in which it was formed; its mission is to revive and preserve the work of modern choreographers and to be a repository of the black tradition in American dance and music. The AAADT is a repertory company, which means it performs the work of many choreographers, not just its founder, to fulfill its mission. In the age where dance combines and synthesizes the ideas of many people, the AAADT brings together the creative energies of many African American choreographers.

Paul Taylor

Paul Taylor (1930-) was born in Pennsylvania. Like Ted Shawn and José Limón before him, Paul Taylor did not begin his young adult life as a dancer. He studied painting in college and was a competitive swimmer. His love of art and physicality eventually were combined as he began to study dance in his early 20s. Taylor's gifts did not take long to develop, and by the mid-1950s he was a soloist with the Graham Company. Never one to be satisfied with one technique only, Taylor was a guest artist with the New York City Ballet as well. This eclecticism is the hallmark of Taylor's choreography and what makes him the clearest example of the fusion of styles so typical of the latest generation of modern dancers. No two Taylor dances look alike. He has created works to classical music with an athletic, plotless, and graceful movement vocabulary, such as *Esplanade* (1975); dances to popular music that involve pedestrian movements and social dance, such as *Changes* (2008); and dark narrative dramas to commissioned modern music, such as *Big Bertha* (1971). His dances cover a remarkable range of topics, dance styles, and music choices. Taylor's versatility is emblematic of the variety of choices available in today's world. Global society provides exposure to a huge range of ideas, and the modern dance of Paul Taylor reflects this.

Twyla Tharp

Twyla Tharp (1941-) was born in Indiana. Tharp studied a variety of dance and music styles as a young woman and then moved to New York to study dance at Barnard College. She joined the Paul Taylor Company after graduation, but it was not long after that she began making her own dances. Tharp's work is known for its use of large expanses of space, a clear sense of timing and musicality, and often the element of surprise. These choreographic surprises come from the combination of movements that Tharp puts together. She describes her movements as coming from ballet, jazz, boxing, and her own invention. Dance critic Deborah Jowitt describes the style as "acquiring a strong classical technique and then learning to fling it around without ever losing control" (Mazo, 1977, p. 312). Tharp's choreography is performed by many dance companies, most notably the Twyla Tharp Dance Foundation and Hubbard Street Dance Chicago. In addition to concert dance, her work has been seen on Broadway in shows like *Singin' in the Rain* (1985) and *Movin' Out* (2003) and in films such as *Hair* (1978) and *Amadeus* (1984). Her work in film and on Broadway has helped to spread the popularity of her style in combining unusual movement vocabularies together while maintaining an overall sense of theatricality and athleticism.

1980-2000: Collaborators

By now the art form of modern dance is nearly a century old. Most of the pioneers have passed away. The society in which modern dance exists begins to include dances transmitted electronically over the Internet or interacting with new media. New forms such as dance theater and postmodern dance have begun to gain recognition. For modern dance, the last 20 years of the 20th century were a time of collaboration in the creative process (see table 7.5). While dance has always been a collaborative medium, relying on the talents of many dancers, costumers, set and lighting designers, and choreographers to make its art, this is a new kind of collaboration. Choreographers begin to use the movements and experiences of the dancers themselves to create their work. In the generation of the pioneers, the feelings and ideas of the central choreographer of a company were the subject of the dances. By the end of the century, the collaborative ideas of the dancers became a driving force in many choreographers' creative processes. The work of two of the most acclaimed modern dance companies of the next generation, Pilobolus and Bill T. Jones, are prime examples.

Pilobolus

Pilobolus Dance Theatre was founded by six students at Dartmouth College in 1971, all pupils of dance composition taught by Alison Chase. Although founded before 1980, the company did not come to its status as an innovator until the very late 1970s and early 1980s. In that period, they established a new and unique style of modern dance. The work can be described as moving human sculpture making, done to create clever and startling visual effects, often with a sense of humor. The surreal anthropomorphic picture making that marks their choreography has spawned an entirely new style of modern dance, now in practice by other companies, such as Momix, founded by one of the original Pilobolus creators Moses Pendleton. Pilobolus is not only popular on the dance concert stage but also in high demand as public entertainment. They have had notable performances at the opening of the 2002 Olympic Games and on the televised Academy Awards ceremony.

Table 7.5 Significant Events From 1980 to 2000

1981	First space shuttle orbital flight. MTV begins. First reported cases of AIDS.
1982	Michael Jackson's *Thriller*.
1983	Bill T. Jones/Arnie Zane Dance Company is formed.
1985	First use of DNA typing.
1986	Space Shuttle *Challenger* disaster. Chernobyl disaster.
1988	Fall of the Berlin Wall.
1989	Pilobolus choreographs *Particle Zoo*.
1990	Sir Tim Berners-Lee invents World Wide Web. Bill T. Jones choreographs *Last Supper at Uncle Tom's Cabin/The Promised Land*.
1991	First website is launched.
1993	First smart phone is introduced.
1994	End of apartheid and election of Nelson Mandela as president of South Africa. Bill T. Jones choreographs *Still/Here*.
1996	First successful cloning creates Dolly the sheep.
1997	Princess Diana dies. First Harry Potter book published. Pilobolus choreographs *Elysian Fields*.
1998	Google is founded.
1999	Euro is introduced. Columbine massacre. Pilobolus creates *Last Dance* on the theme of the Holocaust.

It is not only their unique style of moving that makes Pilobolus so remarkable but also the process by which they create their work. There is no one central choreographer for the company; their work is created collaboratively through group improvisation. Listings of choreographers in their programs include all of the dancers present when the work was originally made. In recent years, Pilobolus has created a project titled the International Collaborators Project, in which they invite outside artists to add new ideas into their unique collaborative creative process.

Bill T. Jones

Bill T. Jones (1952-) was born in Florida. His major choreographic work began as a duet company with Jones' partner Arnie Zane in 1983. Most of the repertory

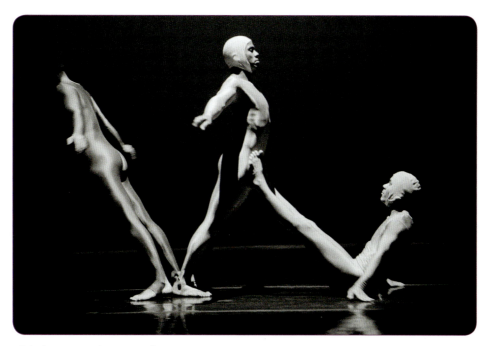

Pilobolus Dance Theatre performance, 1996.

created by Jones for his 10-member company involves evening-long dances dealing with sociopolitical and personal issues. These works are interdisciplinary in nature, often accompanied by text as well as music. His highly regarded *The Last Supper at Uncle Tom's Cabin/The Promised Land* (1990) is a work representative of his style. The piece uses pedestrian movement, theatrical and pedestrian costumes, text, music, dance movement, and a variety of body types to explore issues of racism in our time. Similarly, Jones' landmark work *Still/Here* (1994) uses the life experiences of participants in survivor workshops that Jones held with people who had life-threatening illnesses in 11 different cities. Jones' work is created through a discovery process, where participants tell their stories to Jones through both words and movements. The text and movement are then edited and shaped by Jones into a highly polished, emotionally charged work of dance theater. Jones' work encapsulates the collaborative creative style of this generation of modern dance, and the very issues on which he creates dances are emblematic of the times in which Jones choreographs.

DANCE IN HIGHER EDUCATION

As a student of dance, you are connected to the history of dance in two ways. The first is that the techniques you are learning in the studio are direct descendants of the techniques described in this brief history. Many of them have remained virtually unchanged since their creation by the pioneers of the art form. Many classes in colleges and universities, however, are not one set technique. Teachers today tend to combine exercises that they have learned from various styles they have encountered in their training, often inventing their own versions of these.

Dance students are connected to the history of modern dance in another way. The existence of dance in university settings was integral to the development of the art form. The summer festivals where Hanya Holm, Martha Graham, Doris Humphrey, and Charles Weidman developed their work and honed the aesthetics of modern dance were held at Bennington College in Vermont. In fact, a large part of the touring schedule of the Humphrey and Graham companies, even as early as the 1930s, involved stops at college campuses. University dance programs have supported the work of some of the greatest choreographers of this century and continue to employ guest artists as a mainstay of their programs.

Although modern dance was rarely commercially successful, it became institutionalized at colleges and universities. It fit the intellectual, artistic, and physical demands of the growing population of women in higher education beginning in the late 1920s, and it simultaneously became a place where professional dancers could find employment and where choreographers could create works exploring political and social change without the concerns of financial viability.

A parallel and intersecting story to the development of modern dance in education is the development of physical education curriculum in higher education, especially for women. From the early part of the 20th century, physical education teachers began to teach what they called aesthetic calisthenics, or later aesthetic dance, as part of the curriculum for physical and mental well-being for women. The late-19th-century educator Melvin Gilbert designed this as the centerpiece of women's college physical education experiences. His student Gertrude Colby began to use Gilbert's work as well as experiment with natural rhythmic movement with children. Colby taught at Columbia University in New York. At the same time, Bird Larson, a colleague of Colby's at Barnard College and a student of the Delsarte method, also began experimenting with natural rhythmic movement expression with music. She synthesized these ideas with her background in corrective physical education to develop a scientifically based approach to dance technique. Margaret H'Doubler, a women's physical education teacher from the University of Wisconsin, went to New York in 1917 for professional development and encountered this method. Both Colby and Larson were in New York teaching these methods when H'Doubler arrived. While H'Doubler was studying in New York, she was exposed to the work of the very early modern dance, or new dance, pioneers, including Isadora Duncan. She found a kinship between the goals of early modern dance and the goals of aesthetic dance in physical education. Both modern dance and aesthetic dance in physical education used movement to strengthen and empower women and to lead to self-actualization, or self-fulfillment. From these methods and beliefs, H'Doubler founded the first dance major in higher education at the University of Wisconsin in 1926.

This history also explains why many kinds of modern dance techniques became a part of college curriculum. While not all forms of modern dance are taught with equal frequency, and the eclectic class is probably the most common, many of the pioneers and second-generation students of the pioneers had strong connections to college dance programs. Their voices are still represented through the movement vocabularies, training exercises, and philosophies used today.

RELEVANCE OF MODERN DANCE TODAY

Throughout the history of modern dance, there have been three constants. The artists of every generation of the art form have responded to the times in which they lived through creation of movement. In every time period, modern dance has resisted the traditions of the past. And the artists of modern dance in every era have consistently reevaluated the purpose and significance of the art form. All of these ideas and forces are still relevant today. While the issues of the day are not the same as they were when the pioneers were connecting to the modernist movement in art, modern dance has the breadth and versatility as a genre to respond to the present. As dance critic Marcia B. Siegel (1969, p. 4) so eloquently reflects, "What's modern about modern dance is its resistance to the past, its response to the present, and its constant redefining of the idea of dance."

Many dance historians believe that we have entered a postmodern era in dance. Postmodern dance, born in the 1950s through the movement improvisation workshops of dance greats such as Anna Halprin, thrived in the 1960s when pedestrian movements and everyday objects found their way into dances, just as everyday objects were appearing in pop art, like the famous Campbell's Soup can painting by Andy Warhol. Choreographic collectives, like the artists at Judson Church in New York, began to question the relationship between performers and the audience and between performance and everyday life. The aesthetics of postmodern dance dictated that dance be conceptual. It was to mimic the cerebral quality of modern art. Postmodern dance is a close cousin to modern dance, and in our current era of global fusion there is no distinct line between the two. Some postmodern ideas and movement vocabulary have begun to be part of the lexicon of modern dance, and vice versa. Perhaps a decade from now someone will write that the generation of 2000 to 2020 was characterized by a blurring of the lines between all genres of dance. In its constant struggle to redefine dance itself, modern dance could embrace this idea.

Many people believe that the terms *contemporary dance* and *modern dance* are synonymous. For the purposes of this text, there is a distinction between the two. The term contemporary means any dance that is happening in the time period in which you are living. So contemporary ballet, contemporary modern, and contemporary jazz exist. If you were living in 1925, Isadora Duncan would be doing contemporary dance. Modern dance, on the other hand, refers to the family tree of styles that reflect the modern dance genre and its aesthetic values. Chapter 8 details the aesthetics of five of the major styles of modern dance that are still taught as distinct techniques today.

SUMMARY

The history of modern dance is tied to the social, political, and artistic trends of the era in which it was created. Beginning as new dance in the early part of the 20th century, modern dance was shaped by the women's movement, new trends in visual arts, and a growing love of the scientific approach. The matriarchal generation of Isadora Duncan, Loie Fuller, and Ruth St. Denis inspired the imaginations of the dance world as it pulled away from the traditions of the previous century.

As each era of the 20th century changed, so did modern dance. The 1920s to 1930s were the pioneering era of the art form. Luminaries like Martha Graham, Doris Humphrey, and Katherine Dunham began to shape and define what this new genre of dance would be. The 1940s and 1950s, the period of successors to the pioneers, gave rise to such new stylistic variations through the work of artistic giants such as José Limón and Merce Cunningham. From 1960 through the 1980s, choreographers and dancers synthesized and reexamined the work of the pioneers, bringing new kinds of movement vocabulary to the modern dance idiom. Icons such as Alvin Ailey and Twyla Tharp are emblematic of this time. The last portion of the 20th century brought forward the value of collaboration through the work of truly inventive creators, including Bill T. Jones and Pilobolus.

The contributions of Margaret H'Doubler inspired the innovative design of modern dance curriculum in higher education. Modern dance continues to be a relevant art form for the 21st century. Its uniting characteristics are its response to the times in which it is being created, its resistance to past traditions, and its constant reevaluation of its relevance and significance.

To find supplementary materials for this chapter, such as learning activities, e-journal assignments, and web links, visit the web resource at **www.HumanKinetics.com/BeginningModernDance1E.**

WEB RESOURCE

Chapter 8

Five Major Styles of Modern Dance

Modern dance is an umbrella term covering many distinct kinds of dance techniques rather than one cohesive style of dance. This chapter presents a more in-depth look at five of the styles of modern dance: Humphrey-Limón, Graham, Cunningham, Horton, and Dunham. The differences in these styles explain why the modern dance class you are taking now always begins with floor exercises but the modern dance class you took at your home studio never did. Perhaps your current modern class uses only drum and percussion as accompaniment, but your class last semester used recorded music and followed it very closely. These differences between one modern dance class and another may be explained by understanding the background style of modern dance you are learning. This chapter explains the beliefs behind these styles so that you can get the most from your modern dance class.

The five styles covered in this text represent the most common techniques. Some of these techniques, like Graham, have specifically prescribed exercises to follow, called a syllabus, and are referred to as codified techniques. Some are authored by a pioneer of modern dance, like Humphrey-Limón, but do not have one specified syllabus to follow. For both kinds of modern dance techniques, you will be able to understand the style on a deeper level by clarifying their differences and highlighting the philosophies behind them. This understanding is the first step not only to good execution of the movements but to using them for true artistic expression. Other styles have survived intact from the pioneers, such as the Duncan technique, based on the work of Isadora Duncan, but are less frequently taught in higher education settings. It is impossible to say why some techniques have persisted and others have not. Some of the pioneers were clearer about the methods for passing on the tradition; others wrote their own books or designated successors who were strong teachers. The fact that these five techniques have survived does not mean they are the best ways to learn modern dance, only that they are some of the most distinct. Since these five represent such a diversity of thoughts on what dance is, it is hoped that at least one approach will resonate with the way you move, think, and express yourself.

Each of the five techniques covered in this chapter is examined for their beliefs in four areas:

1. The purpose of dance
2. The dancer's relationship to space and gravity
3. Where movement originates in the body
4. The relationship between dance and music

No matter what specific exercises you do in a technique class, the way in which these exercises are done is really the heart of any technique, not the specific steps themselves. All of the techniques discussed use pliés and contractions, but they are each dealt with differently, depending on the philosophy behind them, for example. Trust your teacher and the thoughts of the founders of each style to guide you.

HUMPHREY-LIMÓN

My entire technique consists of the development of the process of falling away from and returning to equilibrium. . . . Dance movement should be fundamentally dramatic, that is to say, human, not decorative, geometrical or mechanical.

Humphrey, 2008, pp. 6-7

If you love dancing closely with the music and moving fluidly through the space with a sense of falling off balance, you may have an affinity for the Humphrey-Limón style of modern dance. This technique represents the teaching and philosophy of two modern dance pioneers, Doris Humphrey (1895-1958) and José Limón (1908-1972). Doris Humphrey, as you read in chapter 7, studied at the Denishawn School, where she had a variety of dance influences. From this early training and her own beliefs about dance, she began developing a technique for training dancers. Her greatest pupil was José Limón, who joined her in developing the technique and in training dancers and teachers who perpetuated the style. Humphrey's philosophy about dance and life was intertwined with the dance technique itself. This was not only a method for training the body to move; it was also a way of creating dances, responding to music, and expressing one's experiences in the world. Many professional dancers and university faculty have been trained in this technique, and it has been disseminated around the world. The Limón Institute is responsible for licensing the reconstruction and performance of the Humphrey-Limón repertory, but it does not provide a specific training program in teaching the technique. This is in large part because Limón himself believed that the technique should not be completely codified and preserved as is, but it should be adapted by individual teachers to suit the needs of their students.

> ### DID YOU KNOW? ▶▶▶▶▶▶▶▶
>
> Humphrey connected her beliefs to the work of German philosopher Friedrich Nietzsche. He believed the human psyche has two sides. One is rational and intellectual (the Apollonian), and one is chaotic and emotional (the Dionysian). Modern dance, as modern life, Humphrey believed, existed between these two extremes, what she frequently referred to as the arc between two deaths (Humphrey, 2008).

Purpose of Dance

Both Doris Humphrey and later José Limón articulated their theory of dance by teaching classes, choreographing dances, and writing. These artists believed that the purpose of dance was to explore and express the human condition. This is undoubtedly why the famous dance critic John Martin wrote of José Limón that watching him dance was like watching "the transfer through movement of an awareness of heroic vision, of human experience, of poetic perception" (1953, p. SM 19).

One of the principles of this technique is that all movement happens between falling into gravity and recovering from it. This means that the most exciting moments in choreography happen between being on balance, falling off balance, and then recovering equilibrium. This idea also relates to the breath. Movement occurs between the in breath and the out breath. As Humphrey says:

> All movement can be considered to be a series of falls and recoveries; that is, a deliberate unbalance in order to progress, and a restoration of equilibrium for self-protection. Thus is typified the basic life struggle for maintenance and increase. A more dramatic medium, or more inseparable from human experience could hardly be imagined; it is inherently both exciting and relevant. The nearer the state of unbalance approaches the dangerous the more exciting it becomes to watch, and the more pleasurable the recovery. This danger zone, which life tends to avoid as much as possible, is the zone in which the dance largely has its existence. (Brown, Mindlin, & Woodford, 1998, p. 60)

Relation to Space and Gravity

Because of its deep-seated belief that dance is a vehicle for expression of the human condition, modern dancers in the Humphrey-Limón tradition are creatures of the earth. In contrast to the world of ballet, which sees dancers as creatures of the air and values the illusion of flight, modern dance in the Humphrey-Limón style acknowledges gravity as the source of humans' connection to the earth and a source of strength, not a force to be defied. Another dance critic said the following after seeing the work of José Limón:

> One of the outstanding characteristics of modern dance is the use of gravity as a force. The floor is a strong base from which the dancer rises to great heights, only to return and rise again. The interplay of vertical movements is a breathing quality which infuses the dance with life itself. (Lewis, 1984, p. 35)

Limón dancer Daniel Lewis (1984, p. 35) would later say that the Limón technique was about "exploring the full spectrum of movement that exists between freedom from gravity and complete subservience to its power."

Origin of Movement

As with most styles of modern dance, movement originates in the pelvis and spine. You will probably hear the phrase *moving from your core* or *centrally initiated movement* in a Humphrey-Limón-based class. This means that the muscles of your abdomen, which help you to maintain balance, are engaged in nearly every movement. You can expect this from a technique whose central aesthetic is related to falling off and regaining balance.

The tension occurring between fall and recovery often leads to emphasizing long diagonal movements, what teachers in this technique call diagonal tensions in the body (figure 8.1). For example, while your left foot is rooted to the floor, the right arm may be reaching away from gravity. Both the energy downward and the energy upward are given equal importance in this style.

From the perspective of this technique, the body is analogous to an orchestra. In this analogy developed by José Limón, each section of the body is like a section of the full orchestra. Each must have some attention paid to it because each plays a role in the overall work; however,

Figure 8.1 Diagonal tension in Humphrey-Limón technique.

there will be times when the violins play the strongest or the trumpets take over the melody. Similarly in the Humphrey-Limón style, your teacher will emphasize which part of the body should be the most noticeable in a movement. She may tell you the arms are the leading instrument, or the chest, for example. Listen carefully and you may hear your teacher refer to the part of the body that you need to "let sing" or "let speak." This is a direct connection to this concept that many teachers well versed in the technique will use.

The emphasis on fall and recovery leads to many bending, turning, and falling movements in this style. Allow yourself to really fall off balance and regain it to get a full feeling for this technique. Many dancers who are new to the style find it difficult to embrace the idea of really losing control and falling. Remember, though, that every fall has a recovery, so the thrill of falling slightly out of control is part of the energy of this style. Some small risk taking is a part of the excitement of this kind of dance.

Doris Humphrey defined all movement as having one of three qualities: sharp accents, sustained flow, and rest. You can expect to see all three of these kinds of movements in a Humphrey-Limón-inspired class. In fact, you will see these qualities not only in the final combination or across-the-floor work at the end of each class but also right from the beginning of the warm-up exercises. Dancers in this style are encouraged to find these moments of sustained connection and sharp accents throughout the class. One way in which these movement differences are emphasized is through breathing. Humphrey-Limón classes will often mention that a movement is done on an exhale or an inhale, and sometimes even the breath pattern for an entire phrase of movement will be discussed.

Relationship to Music

Followers of the Humphrey-Limón technique believe that there is a very close relationship between dance and music. Dances choreographed by both Humphrey and Limón were to music, sometimes commissioned scores, but more frequently extant music. In dances such as *A Choreographic Offering* (1964), which Limón choreographed as a tribute to his teacher Doris Humphrey, Limón used the music score "A Musical Offering" by Johann Sebastian Bach. Many of the thematic introductions of dance phrases coincide with the introduction of musical phrasing, and Limón is reputed to have said that "Mr. Bach" was telling us what to do. In *Mazurkas* (1958), a pianist is featured on stage and acknowledged as part of the dance, showing the respect and connection that music has in the Humphrey-Limón tradition. Many titles of Limón dances, such as *The Moor's Pavane* (1949) and *The Waldstein Sonata* (1975), even contain the name of the music or type of music that is danced to in the title.

Although this style represents a close relationship between music and movement, Doris Humphrey made it clear that the expressive content of the dance was the main reason for creating a work, not the music itself. In *The Art of Making Dances* (1959, p. 23), Humphrey exhorts all choreographers to remember that "The choreographer is the sensitive and willing listener, but not the slave of the composer." She recommends that choreographers be musically literate, knowing the organization of music and its history, so that appropriate music can be selected and so that communication between dancer and accompanist is clear. This does not make the music the motivation for dancing, however.

MARTHA GRAHAM

The function of dance is communication. . . . By communication is not meant to tell a story or to project an idea, but to communicate experience by means of action . . . out of this came a different use of the body as an instrument, as the violin is an instrument. Body is the basic instrument, intuitive, instinctive. As a result an entirely contemporary set of technics was evolved.

Brown, Mindlin, & Woodford, 1998, p. 50

Probably the most iconic image of modern dance in the general public is of a woman clad in a dark leotard and tights seated on the floor reaching upward with her torso curving backward or while standing on one leg with her other limbs outstretched and her focus downward. These are images from the Martha Graham (1894-1991) technique. They are two of her signature movements: the contraction and strike pose, respectively. For many people, modern dance is synonymous with the work of Martha Graham. Known for her theatricality, severity, solemnity, and emotionally charged dances, Graham was a true original. The mythic content of her work was introspective in its involvement with human emotions and the personal exploration of deep-seated motivations. Graham herself described her dances as stylized to represent the times in which she was creating: "Life today is nervous, sharp and zigzag. It often stops in mid-air. That is what I aim for in my dances" (Mazo, 1977, p. 161).

In addition to the power and originality of Graham's choreography, she was known for developing a codified system of exercises that could be used to train dancers in her style. Much of that syllabus comes to us today directly from Graham, and in many places is still taught in precisely the same manner. Graham believed that the first task when working with students "is to teach them to admire strength—the virile gestures that are evocative of the only true beauty. To try to show that ugliness may actually be beautiful if it cries out with the voice of power" (Mazo, 1977, p. 162). It was this admiration of powerful gesture that often gave the work an angular and stylized appearance. But it is not true that lyricism or nuanced movement is not valued in the technique. Graham developed her technique over time and softened some of the exercises to ensure that the movements were not overly rigid.

Purpose of Dance

Graham took a psychoanalytic viewpoint on dance. She believed that the purpose of dance is to illuminate the life and struggles of the human experience, paying particular attention to humans' inner nature. Her dances were dramatic expressions of the conflict between the individual and society in an attempt to look at the internal motivations of humanity. Graham believed that using dance for that purpose would bring psychoemotional enlightenment. In 1938, Graham wrote that "Art is the evocation of man's inner nature. Through art we find man's unconscious—race memory—is the history and psyche of the race brought into focus" (Brown, Mindlin, & Woodford, 1998, p. 50).

Since the purpose of dance is to translate emotional experience in physical form, in the Graham technique, every movement must have a clear and perceivable meaning. This does not mean the movements must be realistic, only that the stylization must be meaningful and recognizable to the viewer as well as to the performer. Graham was clear on this principle: "Everything that a dancer does, even in the most lyrical thing, has a definite and prescribed meaning" (Mazo, 1977, p. 189). Further, she believed that the clear training of the dancer gave a freedom to the dancer's ability to express the emotions and ideas of the choreographer. In Graham's own words, training was the key to articulation: "If you have no form, after a certain length of time you become inarticulate. Your training only gives you freedom" (Mazo, 1977, p. 157). Thus the rigor of your training was all part of the purpose of the art form—and Graham believed in rigorous training! Her demand for total discipline and attention during class, and her anger when this was not accorded her, are well documented. While the movements in the technique itself are not natural gestures, they are artificial ones; the inner commitment to them and the emotional sincerity of the dancers presenting them are entirely real.

Relation to Space and Gravity

The Graham technique has a clear relationship to the floor and to gravity. Like Humphrey-Limón, Graham dancers are creatures of the earth who respect the power of gravity. However, unlike the previously discussed technique where the power to pull away from gravity gives you energy and a search for equilibrium, the Graham technique believes that the fall is the acknowledgment of the power of gravity. Many of the exercises in the Graham syllabus require the dancer to fall powerfully into the floor, and these movements are seen repeatedly throughout the Graham repertory. To Graham, this was not just a physical act; it was a psychological one. "We teach the falls to the left because, unless you are left-handed, the right side of the body is the motor side; the left hand is the unknown. You fall into the left hand—into the unknown" (Mazo, 1977, p. 157). The exploration of the space of the stage, including the floor itself, is part of the emotional content of the technique.

Because space can reveal emotional content, according to Graham, the set is an integral part of the ability of a dance to communicate. When Graham's choreography took on huge mythic subjects, such as in the dances *Clytemnestra* (1958) or *Night Journey* (1947), they used the entire expanse of the stage. When they were particularly introspective, as in *Errand into the Maze* (1947) or *Lamentation* (1930), the use of the stage space was minimal. Space itself is part of the emotional landscape of a Graham dance.

Origin of Movement

According to Martha Graham's philosophy, movement is generated from three places: the action of contraction and release, the pelvis, and the emotional inner self. The contraction, or strong pulling back and curving of the torso, and the release of this movement by returning to a straight torso are symbolic of the dichotomies in life. It is the contrast between desire and duty, between fear and courage, between weakness and strength.

The repeated use of the contraction and release gives a rhythmic energy to the movements in this technique, and its execution is central to the seated, lying, and standing exercises of the training method (figure 8.2). The torso and pelvis, in this way, are the central focus of the movement, while the arms and legs move in concert with the spine.

The series of exercises known as spirals, done seated in fourth position, is an excellent example of how the pelvis, rooted to the floor and drawing its energy from this proximity, is the first part of the body to move (figure 8.3).

Graham taught students that the hip bone should move as a jewel in a watch movement. This makes the pelvis the point of stability and the motivator of the movement. A clear articulation of the pelvis will definitely result from your study of this style of modern dance. Whether the movement begins with a contraction of the torso or a movement of the hip bone, it must be done with strength. Both lyrical and dramatic movement must be equally strong.

Because of this quality of strength and the importance of intentional meaning behind every movement, you could say that movement in the Graham technique begins in the mind, especially in the dancer's subconscious. In the Graham style, everything is motivated from the inner life. If this is not there, the movements become sterile. As Graham said, "This lack of motivation will lead to meaningless

Figure 8.2 Contraction while seated (a) and standing (b).

movement, and meaningless movement leads to decadence" (Horosko, 2002, p. 75). Every movement in the technique results from an emotional impulse. Graham told her students that if you must mark a movement, mark the physicality but never the dramatic meaning.

Many of the movements in the Graham technique use terms from ballet, such as the numbered positions of the feet and the terms *plié* and *relevé*. When you take a Graham class, you can expect to hear many of these basic terms from ballet used regularly. Although Graham's technique was in many ways a rebellion against ballet, it

Figure 8.3 Spiral.

did, like all of the early modern styles, overlap in some ways with a classical dance vocabulary. There are turned-out as well as parallel movements in the Graham technique. Like a ballet class, the work in a Graham technique class is always in the same order: floor work, breathing, knees, standing center work, barre work, traveling across the floor. While the syllabus has a set order and structure of the exercises, the number of repetitions and whether everything from the syllabus is included in a particular class is up to the individual instructor.

Relationship to Music

Much of what Martha Graham believed about the relationship between dance and music was a result of her longtime association with Denishawn music director Louis Horst. He served as advisor, mentor, and partner to Graham for the majority of her career. He convinced Graham that she should commission music for her dances rather than use already-existing music, a practice she regularly upheld. Graham gave the composer a set script of action, mood, and timing for the work. She listened to sections of score while it was being composed but waited to choreograph the work until the score was completely finished. Horst, and consequently Graham, preferred modern music as the accompaniment to dance.

Whether the music was written specifically for the dance or not, Graham, under Horst's influence, believed that music should be sublimated to the dance. As Horst himself said, "The question is not how great a dance composer is, but what he does for the dance. The composer-accompanist must expect to sacrifice some of his identity as a musician when he writes or plays for the dance" (Mazo, 1977, p. 194). The function of the music was to support the mood and emotional content of the piece, not to be the guiding stimulus for its creation.

MERCE CUNNINGHAM

The dancer strives for complete and tempered body-skill, for complete identification with the movement in as devastatingly impersonal a fashion as possible. Not to show off, but to show: not to exhibit, but to transmit the tenderness of the human spirit through the disciplined action of a human body.

Cunningham, 1997, p. 60

Even in modern dance, an art form of innovators, Merce Cunningham (1919-2009) still stands out as unique. His innovative disassociation of music from dance led to an entirely new way of creating choreography and an entirely new way for audiences to view modern dance. In addition to his nearly 70-year career as a choreographer, Cunningham is the creator of a physically rigorous technique that he used to train dancers to perform in his intellectually intense aesthetic.

While the structures of dances and process of making the choreography are completely unlike anything that preceded it, the movements that make up the dances are not unfamiliar. The Cunningham technique is marked by great speed and clean lines. Some of the lexicon looks like classical ballet; some are pedestrian actions such as walking or running. Dancers trained in the Cunningham style are quite virtuosic. The work, in many ways, looks more akin to the great 20th-century ballet choreographer George Balanchine's style of abstract neoclassical ballet than the work of Martha Graham or any of the other modern dance pioneers. There are long horizontal leaps, bouncing jumps, and sharp angles, all executed with great elegance. There are leans and falls, as in both Humphrey-Limón and Graham styles, but in the Cunningham technique these are usually achieved by one dancer leaning on another without bending from the waist. The style is marked by fast changes in direction and precise, fully committed dancing.

In 1973, *Village Voice* dance critic Deborah Jowitt wrote that she spoke with a child whose school had attended a Cunningham concert. The child described the work as "like the inside of a watch where everything was moving at the same time, but at different speeds and some things affected other things" (Mazo, 1977, p. 230). This is an insightful overview of the experience of seeing the Cunningham company perform.

Purpose of Dance

For Cunningham, dance was not an expression of emotion or of storytelling. Its purpose was not personal or political. It was visual. "Movement itself is expressive, regardless of intentions of expressivity, beyond intention" (Cunningham, 1984, p. 103). This means the very act of moving as a human being was expressive to Cunningham. A choreographer or dancer did not need to superimpose any other meaning on the movements. Cunningham is often quoted as saying that movements don't mean anything, and he openly criticized the Graham technique, in which he was trained, for saying so. Cunningham believed that movement was intrinsically meaningful.

Cunningham dancers perform with intensity and commitment. Their commitment, however, is to make the movement full and the stillnesses complete, not to add a specific human emotion to the movements. This may be difficult for you if you have never taken a Cunningham-style class. Clean performance of steps with complete personal commitment will be required of you, but hold back from trying to perform the movements with a specific emotional quality. Cunningham believed that emotion was present in the dance because it was done by human beings who could not help but to express some of who they are in movement. This was enough meaning.

Choreography by Merce Cunningham has often been likened to the work of abstract expressionist painters, especially Jackson Pollock, whose action paintings consist of drips of paint on a canvas. While both artists leave the viewer with a lot to interpret, this is actually not a completely accurate analogy. Pollock, like all the abstract expressionists, believed the body was a source of expression and that abstraction would get us back to our most primitive, true, emotional selves. Cunningham was not looking for the deep-feeling self. He believed the emphasis for both dancer and the audience should be seeing deeply, not feeling deeply.

Cunningham's work is visually complex. Many things seem disassociated, but then the viewer finds unpredictable connections. This has been likened to the feeling of contemporary urban life. Dance, for Cunningham, reflected the modern way of life, not the primitive subconscious. He saw people as separated by the quick speed at which they are moving and acting, although this separation could end at the very next moment that they turn around and do things together. This is a frequent occurrence in a Cunningham dance.

He was also interested in how the pace of technology was changing the pace of daily life and personal rhythms. He considered technology to be a partner in the creative process and used LifeForms, computer software, to choreograph several dances. While Cunningham saw his work as evocative of modern interactions, he doesn't tell people what to look at—that is up to them. Cunningham said they should look at the work on their own terms, not his.

Relation to Space and Gravity

The Cunningham technique has a unique relationship to space compared with other modern dance techniques. Rather than identifying clearly strong or important areas on stage, such as the downstage (front) area or center stage, Cunningham decentralized the space. This means that the stage is filled with different actions happening in a number of locations, and there is no one place that is the central focus of the stage. The use of space becomes much less predictable. You can never say exactly where a dancer will be coming from or where she will end up in the space. This enhances the collage effect of the work. Items, such as movement phrases or duets and trios, are put together not necessarily to form one cohesive whole but to create something whose fragments are of equal importance. In this way, the stage space itself relates to the fragmentation of modern urban life. Similarly, there is no hierarchy of dancers in the Cunningham company, no principal dancer, since there is no dramatic action to tell or abstract. Everyone has a solo; everyone is part of the group.

In relation to gravity, Cunningham's work is much more vertical than the other two styles discussed. The long balletic lines of most of the Cunningham vocabulary make this technique look more buoyant and vertical. Gravity is neither support nor a symbol of power; it is simply a physical force on the dancers. The long vertical preference of this technique comes from a frequent use of classical movement. Cunningham believed that using a set vocabulary of artificial movements, such as those found in classical ballet, would liberate the dancers from the limitations of their own instincts. He did not want dancers to invent idiosyncratic movements, which would reveal too much of their personal and emotional states. He was cautious, however, in his use of this vocabulary. He did not want the dancers to look identical, a problem he had seen in ballet before. The "trouble with virtuosity and technique," Cunningham said, "is that the dancers come to rely on them, rather than themselves, and everybody comes out looking the same" (Mazo, 1977, p. 222). This is perhaps why Cunningham infused the classical movements in his dances with pedestrian actions to preserve the individuality of his dancers by widening their movement vocabulary.

While Graham and Humphrey considered their relationship with gravity to be a driving force in creating dance, Cunningham's driving relationship was with the forces of chance. Cunningham developed elaborate charts that covered a range of possibilities for how the movements, phrases, spacing, numbers of dancers, order of the sections, and so on could be arranged in a dance. He then used dice rolling, coin tossing, and other methods of chance operations to determine which of the options became the structure of the dance. He believed that chance added complexity to the work and replaced personal aesthetic decisions. Chance operations took the place of impulses that abstract impressionists, like Pollock, would have ascribed to unconscious motivation.

Origin of Movement

According to the Cunningham technique, the body operates from a point of balance in the lower spine. The back and spine, in fact, are the locus of much of this technique. Cunningham felt that ballet focused mainly on the legs and that modern dance focused on the back and torso. He wanted to connect the two. The back "acts not just as a source for the arms and legs, but in itself can coil and explode like a spring, can grow taut or loose, can turn on its own axis" (Mazo, 1977, p. 205). In class, this translates to the incorporation of classical ballet leg work, with the addition of the parallel position. A Cunningham class begins in center, however, rather than at the barre, because this forces the dancer to focus on the connection of the back and legs more while striving to maintain balance. These exercises develop a new level of coordination of the head, arms, and legs so that they can move quickly. Not unlike George Balanchine, who adapted the classical ballet lexicon to train dancers to move faster in his choreography, Cunningham adapted the classical training exercises of the legs to enhance speed and clarity.

The class begins in the center with exercises intended to reinforce the importance of the connection of the legs and spine. The back is warmed up and then the legs, then both are worked together. Next come twists and tilts of the spine while standing. Cunningham liked to do the spine work standing because it related more closely to the way dancers move in choreography, since they do not do long sections on the floor in most Cunningham work, and it reinforces the verticality of the style.

The Cunningham technique calls for balletic clarity in the feet and legs, with a supple spine and quick turns of the neck. The combination is both fresh and elegant. This technique, in fact, looks more like ballet than any other form of modern dance, largely because of its demand for rapid shifts of weight and changes of direction. Longtime Cunningham company member Carolyn Brown says the training in this technique involves "training the body to move with speed, flexibility and control; to move with the sustained control of slow motion; to move free of any particular style" (Mazo, 1977, p. 205).

Having technical training that is free of style, as Brown mentions in her comment previously, is an important principle to Cunningham. When you are in a Cunningham class, do your best not to stylize or personalize the movement. Aim for clarity and simplicity. While Cunningham did not want automatons moving in unison on stage, he believed the natural differences in dancers would come out without emphasis. All dancers are different in anatomy and temperament, and that is sufficient difference in this technique to make the movement differ from person to person without the external imposition of something else on the work. Freedom from idiosyncratic style is one hallmark of classicism.

Cunningham addressed the fact that class can become repetitious. It is necessary to repeat exercises in any style to achieve mastery. Rather than see this as a chore, Cunningham regarded it as a sort of meditation. This means you will need to give mental attention as well as physical attention to class. Cunningham remarked that a good class should use both intellect and instinct and "put them together so that both are working in unison" (Cunningham, 1984, p. 73).

Relationship to Music

Merce Cunningham shocked the dance world by separating dance and music and declaring that they had no real relationship except to occupy the theater at the same time. It is "hard for people to accept that dancing has nothing in common with music other than the element of time and division of time," Cunningham explained (Brown, Mindlin, & Woodford, 1998, p. 91). But to him, it seemed eminently logical. "You don't need a meter to walk down the street. You stop and go and slow down and speed up, and I take my premise of a human moving from walking. We all walk with the same mechanism, but we all express ourselves differently just by walking. Dancing is simply an extension, in a big way, of walking: if we don't need a metric beat for walking, we don't need it for dancing" (Mazo, 1977, p. 208).

The connection between music and dance, however, even in the Cunningham technique, is not entirely arbitrary. Although the music does not lead the dance or structure it in any way, it has a symbiotic relationship to dance. The score for a Cunningham dance does not exist without the movement. The reason for the creation of the scores to Cunningham's dances was as accompaniment to the performance. These were not already-extant music compositions. In fact, in one notable example, *Signals*, created in 1970, composer Gordon Mumma designed sensor belts worn by the dancers, which produced sound when they moved. In this case, the music was not just created for the dance; it was literally dependent on the dance. The music, most frequently composed by John Cage, followed the same chance operations methods in its creation. There is a shared sensibility between the music and the dance in the Cunningham technique.

According to Cunningham, this separation of music and dance leads to freedom in choreography. The rhythm of the movement can be based on human rhythms, on the rhythms of the dancers executing the movements. The shape and duration of a phrase of dance are determined by the phrase itself, not the outside imposition of the composer's meter. As Carolyn Brown explains, "rhythm comes out of the nature of the movement and the movement nature of the individual dancer" (Mazo, 1977, p. 208). It would be more accurate to say that music and dance in the Cunningham style each give the audience a choice of focus or the opportunity to see connection. It is up to the viewer to decide what is important and what is connected in the work.

Spiral movements of the back are common in the Cunningham technique.

LESTER HORTON

I am sincerely trying now to create a dance technique based entirely on corrective exercises, created with a knowledge of human anatomy . . . a technique having all the basic movement which govern the actions of the body; combined with a knowledge of the origin of movement and a sense of artistic design.

   Warren, 1977, p. 66

Dances by Lester Horton (1906-1953) are experiences of total theater. He used sets, costumes, music, and movement to create his choreographic works, often taking a personal hand in the creation of each element. His dances were rich in imagery and dynamic tensions. Horton was known not only as a powerful narrative choreographer but also as a master teacher. Influenced by Native American culture and many other ethnicities, Horton used a large vocabulary of movements to create his choreography. He saw it as a necessity to train the dancers in his company to be able to execute this movement with clarity and individuality. Horton was greatly assisted in the development of the technique by one of his dancers, Bella Lewitzky, later a choreographer in her own right. Lewitzky brought order and specificity to the style of training, while Horton used his extremely keen sense of observation and his charismatic personality to bear. Horton's goal in the technique was to help each dancer to find what was unique in herself and to bring that out in her movements. The technique avoids specific mannerisms, such as the contraction and release of the Graham technique, and focuses instead on circular movements, oppositional stretches, and lyricism.

Purpose of Dance

The purpose of dance for Lester Horton was personal and political expression. His dances were representational, often inspired by an event or character in history. They were sometimes emotional and sometimes light and entertaining. While they all have theatricality in common, the movements of the dances in the Horton repertory were always changing and growing as Horton found new inspirations. Because of this, he strove to create a dance technique that was not overly stylistic.

   His purpose in developing the technique was to correct and improve on a dancer's physical limitations so that they could pursue a variety of movement alternatives. In addition to disciplining the body, Horton believed in mental commitment from the dancers, encouraging them to dance with meaning and to find themselves in the movement.

   Horton also believed that the dance technique that he created needed to be "truly representative of this great country" (Warren, 1977, p. 66). He used movements based on Native American ritual dance to achieve this goal as well as an open mind for change. Dancers who worked with Horton over an extended period often remarked that dance for him was an ever-changing entity. Horton, a prolific inventor of movement, was well known for never teaching two classes exactly the same way. This is reflected in the fact that even today, although there is a set of specific exercises associated with the Horton technique, the order of exercises can vary based on the teacher's interpretation of the style. The development of individuality and the flexibility to allow for change are part of the Horton principles.

> **DID YOU KNOW?** ▶▶▶ ▶▶▶▶▶▶
>
> Individuality and equality stretched beyond movement choices for Horton. In a time when non-Caucasian dancers were prohibited from taking class in major studios, Horton opened his doors to all dancers. He was interested in Native American mask making and believed humans all wore masks. Race or ethnicity was just one more mask that each person wore. Horton saw it as the job of dance to see beneath the mask.

Relation to Space and Gravity

Many of the movements in the Horton technique came from his fascination with Native American dance. You can see the grounded respect for the earth in his movement and the connection to drum rhythms that emerged from the Native American aesthetic sense. Horton's technique was not just connected to the earth but also to the sky. The movements of the technique are characterized by long lines and lots of level changes; even the floor movements in this style involve extended reaches upward. Many floor combinations are repeated standing as well as seated, and attention is paid to changes in level. In other words, many of the exercises practice the transition from seated to standing. Horton dancer Ana Marie Forsythe explains, "Horton's technique isn't limited to a concept of one or two movements and their contrasts. The technique is dynamic and dramatic, develops both strength and flexibility, and works with an energy that is constantly in motion" (Legg, 2011, p. 84). Much of the power of this technique comes from the rapid and dramatic shifts in the body's elevation derived from Horton's respect for the power of gravity and his love of open sky. To experience the Horton style, particularly the floor work, you can view the *I Wanna be Ready* section of Alvin Ailey's masterwork *Revelations* (1960). Ailey, a student of Horton's and prominent member of his company, based this section on one of the Horton floor exercises.

Additionally, Horton was interested in clearly defined shapes (figure 8.4). The exercises of this technique take dancers through flat backs, lateral reaches, tilts, and lunges. While clean shapes are clearly favored in this style, Horton was concerned not only with the shape of the body but how those shapes can affect the space of the stage. A dancer takes these changing shapes of the body and moves through space with them. This carving of the space creates beautiful negative spaces in the composition of the choreography. This allows the dancer to use the energy of expansive movements as part of the look of the Horton technique. It is not uncommon to see large whole-body movements that move rapidly through the space. While his technique evolved to train dancers without mannerisms, there is still a characteristic expansive use of space in this style of modern dance.

Origin of Movement

There is not one most significant place of origin for all movements in the Horton technique. Rather, this style is more concerned with the idea that you as a dancer become aware of the specific place from which you are moving, which changes depending on the movement itself. In beginning-level Horton classes, many teachers begin working with creating length in the spine and hamstrings, but this is not necessarily the source of all movement in the Horton technique. The energy of movement in this technique comes from the contrast of standing and sitting and from carving the space with expansive shapes in the body. As you become more advanced in this technique, the exercises become longer and more complex. If you were to watch the class, it might look like the dancers are doing short pieces of choreography rather than training exercises. This is why some teachers refer to them as etudes, or small studies, a term used in music.

Figure 8.4 The Horton style often incorporates clearly defined shapes.

While teachers of this technique have leeway in structuring the order of exercises in class, Horton himself began his class standing rather than sitting because, as Forsythe recalls, "Horton believed in getting the body warmed up and blood flowing quickly" (Legg, 2011, p. 84).

As taught by the Ailey School in New York, probably the most well-known place to take Horton classes, the technique has been codified into 17 fortification studies. Each study is aimed at a different skill or area of the body. Class then progresses across the floor with movement phrases, turns, and jumps.

The traditional Horton class, as explained by Joyce Trisler, one of the original Horton dancers, includes movements done on the floor and while standing. This floor work includes transitions to standing or even leaping. Horton moved through the planes of movement, focusing on how the body goes from a low level to a high level and back again. His classes also include studies in elevation, which include falls as well as slow, controlled descents and ascents. His pelvic studies, derived from ethnic movements, are included in every class. The movements of the hands and feet are defined in every exercise, which makes many of the coordination studies quite complex. Although the technique was not intended to produce a dancer in a particular style, Horton class does tend to develop high extensions, fluidity of movement, and limber backs.

Horton balanced his technical training of dancers with an emphasis on lyricism and artistry. He wanted to be sure the exercises in the technique did not become too technical and still allowed for each dancer to develop individuality. One avenue into this sense of lyricism is the flow of one class exercise into another and the flow of one movement into another in each exercise.

Relationship to Music

There is a close relationship between dance and music in the Horton technique. Horton himself was musically talented and even composed some of the music for his dances, so you can expect to follow music in a Horton class. Early in his career, Horton saw the work of Mary Wigman, which was accompanied by simple percussion, and he frequently used a variety of percussion instruments in class, which he was adept at playing himself.

Later in his career, Horton used music to help set the dramatic tone of the dances he was creating. There are both metric and lyric connections to the music in the movement, similar to the relationships in the Humphrey-Limón tradition. In fact, there is a clear emphasis in the technique, even at beginning levels, on developing a sense of musicality. Horton considered a dancer's reaction to the music as an important part of her performance quality. While the choreography in Horton's repertory was inspired by an idea or a theme rather than the music itself, the use of music and the dancers' ability to respond to it are important aesthetics in this style of modern dance.

KATHERINE DUNHAM

My greatest interest in dance had been a subconscious feeling that it was more than a physical exercise; that it was somehow closely related to the people who danced, and naturally I was tremendously excited over the confirmation of this theory which I found in ethnology.

Pierre, 2005, p. 249

Katherine Dunham was interested in the connection between dance and culture. While other modern dancers of her time were examining the connections of dance to the psyche, Dunham was exploring the complex relationship between dance and culture, specifically Afro-Caribbean culture. As a practicing research anthropologist, Dunham was as involved in re-creating Afro-Caribbean culture on stage that reflected the discoveries of her fieldwork as she was in making original dances that commented on the racism and political inequalities of American society. Dunham's early training was in ballet, and both her choreography and her dance technique use some classical movement vocabulary. Her work can be seen as a synthesis of Western classical and Afro-Caribbean movements. There is also an influence from South American, South Pacific, and Mexican cultures in the technique and choreography.

Katherine Dunham was concerned with the prevalent 1930s stereotype that black dancers should dance "naturally" while white dancers should be classically trained. This inspired her to create a specific and codified dance training technique for dancers of all ethnicities. As early as the 1940s, Lavinia Williams, a dancer with Dunham's company, began recording the specific training exercises that Dunham developed and evolved over time. Dunham ran schools in both New York and East St. Louis, influencing many dancers with her methods. Dunham technique is still taught at both the Katherine Dunham Centers for Arts and Humanities in East St. Louis and at the Alvin Ailey School in New York City. Teachers can become certified in teaching the Dunham technique.

In addition to giving dancers professional training, Dunham saw the serious study of dance at her school as proving to inner-city youth, particularly those at her East St. Louis school, that art, culture, and self-knowledge could foster feelings of self-esteem. A political activist all of her adult life, Dunham saw the connections between dance and culture as stretching beyond the stage into the studio, using her training methods to empower youth. Consequently, the technique is based on three philosophical principles: self-knowledge, detachment, and discrimination. Self-knowledge, according to Dunham, means to use movement to look within yourself and learn personal survival as both an artist and a person. Detachment, in this context, means to strip away your ego and be totally invested in the movement itself. Discrimination means to learn when and how to make changes. Following these three principles will make for a dedicated dancer, artist, and citizen of the world.

Purpose of Dance

For Dunham, dance is not just about physical training, but life training. People dance because it both reflects and strengthens life experiences. Dance is a part of cultural heritage and a way to empower individuals as well as groups of people who might otherwise be marginalized by society. Dunham began creating dances at a time in American history when racial segregation was present. Many people had no direct experience with people of other racial backgrounds and therefore no context for viewing her choreography. Because of this, Dunham saw one of the three major purposes of dance as intercultural communication. Dunham's dances sought to connect the anthropological fieldwork she was doing to the stage choreography she created. By seeing re-creations of regional dances from around the world, audiences could gain an understanding and acceptance of others.

Another central idea in Dunham's work was the connection of form and function. Dunham was not just interested in reproducing the movements of dances from the Caribbean; she also wanted to re-create dances that kept their original cultural meaning. Dunham borrowed steps from other cultures in an attempt to bring these cultures to light for other viewers, not to simply add to the style or movement vocabulary of her choreography. Many dances today contain steps originating all over the world but used outside of their original meaning. The Dunham technique preserves the original cultural integrity of the movements by recognizing their origin and meaning within Afro-Caribbean culture.

Another purpose of dance for Katherine Dunham was the idea that the arts are a way to get people actively involved in their communities. She believed that participation in the arts encourages involvement in a community by increasing the ability to communicate with one another. Dunham believed that the more that people are involved in cultural and artistic communication, the more they would be engaged in communities and be prepared to take on civic responsibility. She called this purpose socialization through the arts.

Relation to Space and Gravity

Dunham technique is a training system that integrates traditional material from a cultural context with ballet and other forms of dance that Dunham studied throughout her lengthy career. This means that the aesthetic of the style includes the use of Western classical lines of the body as well as isolations and undulations found in Afro-Caribbean styles. The style includes long body lines and the use of turned-out legs as in ballet. But Dunham felt that while the vocabulary of ballet (her first training) was valuable, it couldn't express all she wanted to say with her dances. Consequently, Dunham technique relies heavily on Caribbean movement as well. A large part of this is a strong grounded way of moving that respects the earth as a source of energy. As in African dance, there is an emphasis on keeping weight down into the floor and having a strong sense of gravity.

Dunham technique has an expansive use of space. Many portions of the class travel across the floor, and combinations at the end of class often travel throughout the space. The space within the body is also an important consideration in this technique. As explained in the next section, attention is focused on multiple centers of movement through the body.

Origin of Movement

Movement in Dunham technique originates in many places in the body, often simultaneously. This is called **polycentrism**. Typical of many African and Afro-Caribbean movement styles, this is a way of dancing where different parts of the body move in different ways at the same time. The torso might move in a circular path while the hips move forward and back. Because of the incorporation of Afro-Caribbean movements, this technique often includes more isolations of the pelvis and undulations of the torso than you might find in other forms of modern dance. Many of the exercises, such as the yonvalou contractions, employ movement that originates in the pelvis or uses the pelvis to support the movement. Jazz dancers often find they are familiar with some of the movements in Dunham technique, especially the isolation exercises.

Dunham technique is often taught in an **accumulation method**. Time is spent ensuring each movement is learned, including its cultural significance and physical nuances. Movements are often rehearsed repeatedly. Eventually movements are combined to create movement phrasing, except perhaps in an advanced class, students will not be asked to perform phrase work without the slow breakdown. A typical Dunham class, according to Albirda Rose Eberhardt, codirector of the Institute of Dunham Technique Certification, has five parts: breathing exercises, barre work, center exercises, progressions across the floor, and a combination.

The class begins with breathing exercises done either in the center or at the ballet barre. This sets the tone for class and begins the focus on breath as a source for movement. Next are a set of barre exercises. Some of these use the traditional ballet barre movements such as tendu and rond de jambe, but many are unique to the Dunham technique. These include flat backs and pressing body weight forward into the barre to build core strength and stamina as well as reinforce good alignment. The third section of class moves away from the barre to the center to work on isolations. These isolations of the torso and pelvis develop strength and articulation. The Dunham technique uses both sharp movements of the torso and pelvis and soft undulating ones, so attention in training these movements is important. The next section of class involves a series of progressions across the floor. These progressions include the unique Dunham walk as well as prances, turns, and jumps, all emphasizing isolation and articulation of individual body parts as well as attention to rhythms. The class ends with a combination, or small dance sequence built from the skills developed in the earlier portions of class.

Relationship to Music

The use of music is extremely important in Dunham technique. Complex musicality is one of its most distinguishing features. The polycentric movement mentioned earlier is set in motion by **polyrhythmic music**, or music that contains multiple rhythms. It is not uncommon in a Dunham class, for example, to have multiple

Learning the coordination of arms and legs in the Dunham technique.

drummers playing. One drummer may be playing a rhythm that can be counted as a 5 or a 7. Another drummer may be playing a 4 or an 8 count at the same time. This makes for exciting energy in the music and the possibilities of moving to different rhythms with different parts of the body. Specific rhythms have been composed not only for Dunham's choreography but also for technique class. This makes for an essential connection between the music and the dance in Dunham technique.

ECLECTIC APPROACH

The five techniques covered in this chapter represent some discrete styles of modern dance that you might encounter in college or university technique classes. What is common, however, is an eclectic approach to modern dance technique. This means that your teacher may be drawing from more than one of the five techniques covered here. The teacher might even bring in other ideas or movement vocabularies from past experience. Since the idea behind modern dance is that it changes with the times, this approach to teaching is not only to be expected but also welcomed. Many instructors chose this way of teaching in part because it reflects changes in contemporary modern dance.

You may wonder why it is important to understand the distinctions between each of the techniques if your teacher will not be teaching one of these five styles purely and will be adding in elements of multiple approaches. The reason is that the more you know about the background of each exercise in class—that is, where it comes from and what it is meant to teach—the more you can gain from your technique class. This understanding will help you to focus on the idea of the exercise. It will also help you to see the larger picture of the philosophies behind modern dance. After all, the point of technique class is not just to do the exercises but also to translate what you have learned in class onto the stage, into choreography, or for personal development. A strong philosophical grounding into the ideas behind the varied techniques in modern dance can help you to accomplish this.

Many modern dance teachers structure their classes based on the way in which they have been trained. As more and more teachers use an eclectic approach, more and more dancers will have this experience. The ideas and movements of many other kinds of dance have begun to come under the umbrella of modern dance in this way, which shows that modern dance is a vital, growing, and contemporary genre.

> ### DID YOU KNOW? ▶▶▶▶▶▶▶
> Modern dance choreography in the 21st century is sometimes referred to as a *bricolage*. This term refers to an assemblage of found objects into a new work of art. In some ways, contemporary modern dance takes already-existing movement vocabularies (the found objects, so to speak) from traditional modern dance (such as Graham and Horton) and assembles it with elements of ballet, improvisation, yoga, and other movement disciplines to make choreography happen. This means that an eclectic approach to training can be a contemporary and valuable one.

Most modern dance classes include a standing center portion, a seated or floor portion, and an across-the-floor portion. An eclectic class is one in which these elements may change from class to class and do not follow a strict or prescribed format, as in an established style of modern. Eclectic classes also may use an exercise directly out of the Graham technique and then use one from the Humphrey-Limón tradition, or the class may include exercises that are invented by your own teacher. There are advantages to this approach. Suppose the teacher wants to strengthen your ability to articulate your spine. She may decide to teach the Graham spiral series on the floor because it has been proven to develop strength and flexibility in the spine. Next, the teacher could have you stand and perform the opening twists of the Cunningham technique so that you can use these newfound articulations while standing. In the combination at the end of class, the teacher may decide to include a Humphrey-Weidman fall to the floor, since this requires a clearly articulating back. In this way your teacher selects proven exercises that will help you develop specific skills.

SOMATIC PRACTICES

Contemporary modern dance choreographers and teachers frequently draw not only from other dance techniques but from other physical practices as well. A teacher may want to use these outside methods to enhance strength or to deconstruct a particular skill. For example, your teacher may want to use the well-tested abdominal exercises from the Pilates method to help you find core strength that you will need to improve balance. Maybe your teacher will use breathing techniques grounded in yoga to develop your understanding of the use of breath in phrasing modern dance combinations.

Many of these alternative physical methods are grouped together under the term *somatic practices* or *body therapies*. **Somatic**, which literally means "of the body," is a term used to describe physical approaches that recognize the importance of the integration of mind, body, and spirit. While this text does not support any one method for providing visual imagery or supportive training methods to dancers or dance teachers, you will benefit from investigating these approaches. The following six approaches are among the most popular support systems for dancers. Each has a unique way of looking at how the mind and body connect and how you can use this information not only to dance more powerfully and clearly but also to improve your movement habits in everyday life.

Alexander Technique

This approach to movement aims at releasing unnecessary muscular tension. The method teaches ways to release tension from overtightening the muscles, which causes the body to become unbalanced or compressed. The goal is to move through the work with a minimum of strain. During an Alexander session, the teacher will observe your posture and movement patterns. She will place her hands on your neck, shoulder, back, or other body part to guide and refine your movements and breath.

Feldenkrais

The goal of the Feldenkrais method is to develop a sensitivity for neuromuscular patterns and rigidity, and expand options for new ways of moving that will aid flexibility and coordination. The Feldenkrais practitioner guides the students through a series of structured movement explorations that involve thinking and imagining while moving. Many of the exercises are based on developmental and everyday movements such as reaching, standing, and sitting. Other exercises are based on a more abstract exploration of how joints and muscles are related.

Trager

The Trager method is system of mind–body education, which consists of both active work, where the client moves, and table work, where the client is passive, similar to massage. The active work is called mentastics. In table work, the Trager practitioner moves the client's body in ways he would move naturally but with a quality of touch that helps the client to experience a sense of moving freely and effortlessly. The intent of the work is to release deep-seated patterns of movement, which may have developed as a result of trauma or illness or the stresses of daily life.

Franklin Method

The Franklin method uses the power of the mind to improve the body's physical functioning. Mind–body connections are approached through a synthesis of Eastern and Western sciences. The method consists of three types of activities: dynamic imagery, which is a multisensory way of using the brain to guide movement; experiential anatomy, which is used to develop physical awareness of the body's design and function; and reconditioning movement, which is an integration of the previous two activities.

Pilates

This is probably the most well known of the approaches reviewed in this chapter. While Pilates is often included as a somatic practice for dancers, it is more of a physical training method than an integrative mind–body approach. Based on the comprehensive work of Joseph Pilates, this method can be taught both as group classes and as one-on-one training sessions. Pilates is an exercise method that uses both mat work and specially designed equipment to strengthen muscles and balance their use in the body. The systematic series of exercises is partnered with focused breathing patterns. The system is an important supplement to dance because it both prevents and rehabilitates injury.

Yoga

Unlike the previously described somatic practices, yoga dates to ancient times, probably the 2nd century BCE. Originating in India, yoga is a spiritual, mental, and physical discipline that is concerned with achieving an enlightened state of being or consciousness through physical practices and meditation. The physical aspects of yoga are quite diverse, and many new and ancient versions, or schools of yoga, exist today side by side. Many dance teachers incorporate asanas, or postures from yoga, such as downward-facing dog, into the movement vocabulary of their dance classes. Others borrow from the pranayama, or breathing techniques that are a part of the practice. Many dancers maintain a separate practice of yoga in addition to their dance technique classes as a way to enhance understanding of themselves physically and to focus on their breathing and concentration.

IDENTIFYING YOUR INSTRUCTOR'S APPROACH

From reading this chapter, you can see that each of the five approaches to modern dance have different exercises as well as different underlying ideas. Just as your teacher selects specific exercises to develop a specific skill, he also selects exercises that teach a philosophy of movement. Dance is not just about physical development; it is about intellectual engagement. You can ask yourself a series of six questions, the answers to which will clarify which philosophy of dance your teacher believes.

1. Where does the instructor start class? Does class frequently begin on the floor or does it start standing in center? Look for Graham and Horton classes to use much more floor work than the other techniques and to begin the floor work earlier than Cunningham technique does.

2. How is the floor used in choreography or across-the-floor combinations? While most modern classes will use the floor for strength and flexibility work, not all will use the floor in choreography. The Cunningham technique will be unlikely to do this, for example. If your teacher is trained in the Graham technique, the floor will be a stopping point for the movement, but if your teacher prefers the Humphrey-Limón style, then she will be likely to use the floor as a springboard for gaining energy. As you recall, the five styles of modern dance have very distinct connections with gravity.

3. What does your teacher say about balance? Humphrey-Limón teachers will encourage you to fall off balance, while Horton and Cunningham classes will encourage you to hold the balance. **Suspension**, or the ability to control the slow peak of your balance, is appreciated by all techniques of modern dance, but the descent from that suspension will be much more dramatic in the Graham style.

4. Where does your teacher say the movement begins? Listen carefully as exercises and movement combinations are explained and keep your eyes open during demonstrations. Don't assume because the exercise looks familiar that you already know how the movement is to be produced. The teacher may want you to imagine that the movement begins in your lower spine, as in the Cunningham style, or she may remind you that the pelvis is the impetus for moving, as in the Graham technique. Some teachers will tell you that a movement begins in your heart, or in a specific emotional intention, particularly in the Graham or Horton technique. The visual imagery that a teacher uses to get you to imagine where and how a movement should be executed is a key to what she finds beautiful or

meaningful in dance. Be sure to include this in your execution of the movement because it is central to your development as an artist and to ensuring what you do in class carries onto the stage.

5. How is music used in the class? In some Cunningham-inspired classes, it is merely background sound, which may or may not influence the specific meter of your dancing. Other classes, particularly those in the Humphrey-Limón and Dunham traditions, will emphasize responding in a personal and visual way to the music through your movement. Traditional Graham classes begin with percussion only.

6. What specific dance terminology comes up in class? Listen carefully for the unique terms that are a part of each specialized form of modern dance. If you hear the terms *fall* and *recovery*, then it is likely there is a Humphrey-Limón sensibility to the class. If your instructor leads quick jumps across the floor that alternate from right to left, you might be in a Cunningham-inspired class. If this same movement has a quick upward-reaching hand motion and the word *sparkle* comes up, you are in a Graham class. If you hear a term you are not familiar with that seems as if it might come from one of these special vocabularies, ask about it. This will give your teacher an opportunity to be transparent about the sources of her class material, something that will help all dancers in the studio.

SUMMARY

The five styles of codified modern dance discussed in this text are Humphrey-Limón, Graham, Cunningham, Horton, and Dunham. Each of these types of modern dance has a different approach to the purpose of dance, the relationship of the dancer to space and gravity, the origin of movement in the body, and the relationship to music. Many teachers do not follow one of these methods strictly but teach an eclectic class that incorporates elements of more than one style. Some classes incorporate other somatic, or body-based, methods of training the body, such as Alexander, Feldenkrais, Trager, Franklin, Pilates, or yoga. The more you can recognize the signature movements and philosophies of the traditional styles of modern dance in the classes you are taking, the more you will be able to learn and enjoy your experiences in a modern dance technique class.

To find supplementary materials for this chapter, such as learning activities, e-journal assignments, and web links, visit the web resource at **www.HumanKinetics.com/BeginningModernDance1E.**

WEB RESOURCE

Glossary

ABA form—A three-section dance structured with two parts, A and B. The first part of the dance, section A, happens twice, repeating after the second part of the dance, section B.

abduction—Moving away from the midline of the body.

accumulation method—Learning small movements very well and then adding on to them as you proceed to the more advanced level.

acute injury—Occurs suddenly during the performance of a physical activity or an injury so severe it prevents performance of a particular movement.

adduction—Moving toward the midline of the body.

aesthetic principles—Rules that govern fundamental beliefs about what is beautiful or satisfying to the senses.

agility—Ability to shift from one movement or position to another quickly and efficiently.

agonist—Contracting muscle. Paired with the antagonist.

Ailey, Alvin (1931-1989)—Founder of the Alvin Ailey American Dance Theatre, which features, develops, and preserves the African American tradition in modern dance. Known for his highly popular, athletic, and musical choreography.

alignment—Positioning of the body for proper performance. Most frequently refers to the arrangement of joints, skeletal system, or spine. Bones are lined up in such a way that weight is transferred through the center of each joint.

anatomical position—Position of the body standing with feet facing forward, hands at sides, and palms forward with thumbs outward.

anatomy—Study of the physical structures of the body.

antagonist—Relaxing muscle. Paired with the agonist.

anterior—Front of the body or front of a part of the body.

arch—Movement of the upper body in which the shoulders curve backward and the chest and sternum lift upward.

arclike—Arm or leg movement in which the limb moves as one piece, traveling a curved path in space.

arm swing—Movement in which the arm falls in response to gravity either from high to low or from side to side.

artistic voice—Each person's unique ability to explore issues and ideas in the world through abstract conceptualizations.

augmentation—To add on to a phrase of movement.

balance—The equal or logical treatment of rest and action in a dance.

basic locomotor movements—Seven fundamental ways of traveling through space: walk, run, hop, jump, slide, gallop, and skip.

battement tendu—Extension of the foot to a full point while keeping the knee straight and the foot in contact with the floor.

body composition—Muscle, fat, bone, and other tissues that make up the total weight of a person.

body swing—Movement of the upper body either forward and back or side to side that responds to the momentum of gravity.

bound flow—Movement that is tight, constricted, or easily stopped.

cardiorespiratory endurance—Measure of stamina and efficiency of the heart and lungs.

chaîne turn—Turn on alternating feet that completes one revolution every two steps.

chassé—Traveling pattern of step–together–step, where the lead foot is met with the opposite foot, and then the lead foot is extended a second time. The first step is with a bent knee, followed by feet that meet in the air in the middle of this step.

choreographic structure—Architecture of a dance. The overall framework for creating the dance that organizes the motifs and phrases that you develop.

chronic injury—Injury that is constant or recurring in the same part of the body over an extended time.

circumduction—Movement that travels in a complete circle.

concentric muscle action—Muscle shortens as it exerts force.

contemporary—From current time. Dances in this style often incorporate elements of modern dance, ballet, jazz, and hip-hop to appeal to the aesthetic preferences of today's viewers.

contraction—Strong movement in the center of the body (torso) that binds the abdominal muscles and curves the spine.

contrast—The differentiation of a movement so that it stands out in some way or the use of differing movements to add variety to a dance.

coordination—Integration of the nervous and muscular systems to perform harmonious body movements.

counterpoint—Dancers doing different things at the same time in choreography.

countertension—Giving equal energy to two parts of the body that oppose one another, such as the arm and leg. You are using these two parts of the body, in effect, to work together by pulling apart from one another. Can also be two dancers giving each other equal dynamic energy.

creative process—Exploration for unique solutions to complex problems, including creating works of art, new inventions, ideas, or strategies.

Cunningham, Merce (1919-2009)—Second-generation pioneer of modern dance. Known for his use of chance operations in creating choreography and for separating the connection between music and dance in creating his works. Also an innovator in the use of dance and technology.

dégagé—Like a tendu, but the foot disengages from the floor to point and the knee remains straight.

Delsarte, François (1811-1871)—French music teacher who developed a system for bodily expressiveness that became widely popular in the beginning of the 20th century as a form of exercise and expression.

demi-plié—Bending of the legs with partial flexion of the knees.

développé—Similar to a battement, except that rather than keeping the knee straight throughout the movement, you unfold the leg from the knee.

dimensional planes—Three planes of space that intersect at the center of personal space, or kinesphere: horizontal (table) plane, vertical (door) plane, and sagittal (forward-and-back or wheel) plane.

diminution—To make a phrase of movement smaller.

direct movements—Gestures or movements in which the path of the body or body part is straight and clear. The opposite of indirect.

Duncan, Isadora (1877-1927)—One of the matriarchs of modern dance. Known for her natural gesture and dance technique of music visualization. Her works included simple movements to express basic emotions.

Dunham, Katherine (1909-2006)—A pioneer in representing the African American voice in modern dance. Her choreography and technique were based on Caribbean cultural dances.

dynamic anatomy—Study of the structure of the body and how it moves. Combines elements of the fields of anatomy and kinesiology.

eccentric muscle action—Muscle lengthens as it exerts force.

embellishment—To elaborate on a phrase by adding aspects to the movement.

en croix—Movement of the legs in the shape of a cross: front, side, back, side.

extension—Increasing the angle of a joint.

fifth position of the arms—Both arms are held overhead with a slight curve to the wrist and elbow. The middle finger of the hand is lined up with the hairline of the forehead or slightly back of that position.

fifth position, or turned-out fifth—Position of the feet and legs where the legs are rotated outward and one foot is placed so the heel of the forward foot is placed against the big toe of the opposite foot.

first position of the arms—Both arms down at the sides of the torso in a slight curve.

first position on the floor—A position in which the dancer is seated with both legs extended in front, and a straight back forming the body into a right angle.

first position, or turned-out first—Position of the feet and legs where the heels remain together and the toes and legs from the hip face outward as close to 180 degrees as possible.

flexed foot—Toes face upward, forming a right angle at the ankle.

flexibility—Ability to move muscles and joints through their full ranges of normal motion.

flexion—Decreasing the angle of a joint.

flow—Quality of continuity in a movement. In Laban terms it can be free or bound.

forced arch—A position in which the dancer has lifted heels and is balancing on the ball of the foot similar to relevé, but with the knees bent.

fourth position of the arms—One arm is held at a 90-degree angle to the side of the torso, the second arm is held above the head. Both arms have a slight curve at the elbow and wrist.

fourth position on the floor—Seated position with the forward leg bent and parallel to the mirrors or front wall of the studio and the second leg at a right angle to it, with the forward foot touching the knee of the second or back leg. Can be done to both sides.

fourth position, or turned-out fourth—Position of the feet and legs where the legs are rotated outward and one foot is placed so the heel of the forward foot is one foot length distant from the big toe of the opposite foot.

free flow—Movement that is continuous and difficult to stop. The opposite of bound flow.

Fuller, Loie (1862-1928)—One of the matriarchs of early modern dance. Used the manipulation of fabric under colored electrical lights to create images from nature.

gallop—Traveling through space forward by alternating opening and closing the legs and feet. One of the seven basic locomotor skills.

genre—Large category of artistic creations based on form, style, and subject matter. Examples of major genres of dance are ballet, modern, jazz, and hip-hop.

Graham, Martha (1894-1991)—A pioneer of modern dance. She was known for her dramatic style of performance and for the development of the Graham technique, in which she developed the ideas of contraction and release.

grande plié—Bending of the legs with deep flexion of the knees.

grapevine—Pattern of walking sideways where the feet alternate crossing in front and behind.

health-related fitness—Muscular strength and endurance, flexibility, and body composition.

Holm, Hanya (1893-1992)—German modern dancer who brought Wigman's ideas to the United States and founded the Hanya Holm School of Dance in New York.

hop—Jumping up and down on one foot. Weight does not transfer from one foot to another. One of the seven basic locomotor movements.

horizontal plane—Also known as the table plane. (Think of wiping off the crumbs on a table.) This plane involves side-to-side (horizontal dimension) and some forward-and-back movements.

Horton, Lester (1906-1953)—Founder of the Horton technique and the Horton Dance Company, the first fully racially integrated American dance company.

Humphrey, Doris (1895-1958)—A pioneer of modern dance and cofounder of the Humphrey-Limón technique. She developed the concept of fall and recovery and was the first to write about choreographic principles in modern dance.

hyperextension—Extending past natural position, such as bending backward.

iconoclast—Person who goes against the trend and develops new and significantly different ideas or behaviors.

improvisation—Asking the dancers to create movements of their own invention. The request is usually structured in some way or follows specific guidelines

indirect movements—Gestures or movements in which the path of the body or body part is wavy or multidirectional. The opposite of direct.

isometric muscle action—Muscle neither shortens nor lengthens as force is exerted.

Jones, Bill T. (1952-)—Contemporary choreographer and dancer known for creating work with socially and politically charged themes.

jump—Hopping up and down on both feet at the same time. One of the seven basic locomotor movements.

kinesiology—Study of the body in motion.

kinesphere—Space around each person that extends as far as you can reach in every direction.

kinesthetic sense (proprioception)—Ability to put together sensory input and past experience to guide your body in movement. This is the sense that allows you to imitate movements you see and to move based on imagination.

Laban movement analysis—A system for understanding and describing all bodily movement developed by Rudolf von Laban in the early part of the 20th century. This method is still in active use today.

Laban, Rudolf von (1879-1958)—Hungarian-born actor and ballet director who created a system for analyzing and recording the specific ways in which the body can move.

labile—Being off balance; a lack of equilibrium.

lateral—Part of the body farthest from the midline of the body.

leap—Jumping as you transfer your weight from one foot to the other while travelling through space.

leg swing—Movement of the leg from high to low, from low to high, or from side to side, which responds to the momentum of gravity.

level—Dancer's distance from the floor in motion or at rest. Described as high, middle, or low.

ligament—Tissue that attaches bones to other bones.

light—Movement that has less apparent effect of gravity in the weight effort. The opposite of strong.

Limón, José (1908-1972)—Mexican-born modern dance choreographer and dancer of the second generation. Developed the Humphrey-Limón technique with his teacher Doris Humphrey, and founded the José Limón Dance Company.

locomotor—Movements that travel through space, such as stylized walking or running, skipping, hopping, galloping, sliding, jumping, leaping, and turning.

lyrical—Fluid, done with a sense of continuous flow. Movement that is not sharp or broken up. Some studios and competitions label choreography or classes with this title. In that context, it can refer to a fluid style of modern dance or a fluid style of modern ballet done without pointe shoes.

macronutrients—Chemical bonds in food that provide fuel for the body. They consist of carbohydrate, protein, and fat.

marking—Doing a movement sequence smaller or with less intensity. This can be done to review and aid memory without exhausting the dancer or to keep the dancer safe in the case of injury.

masterwork—An artistic creation that most clearly represents the era, genre, society, or artist who created it.

medial—Part of the body closest to the midline.

meter—The rhythm of the music, especially how the beats are divided into measures.

mindfulness—State of mind where you are open to new information, multiple perspectives, and new ways of thinking, including thinking about behaviors you have executed before. This term was coined by Harvard psychologist Ellen Langer.

mindlessness—State of thinking where rote habit takes over.

motif—Small section of movement that expresses a central idea or theme of the dance.

movement phrase—"Sentence" of dance or a grouping of meaningful movements. Usually larger than a motif.

movement vocabulary—Specific steps, gestures, and shapes of the body that make up the dance. The building blocks of a particular dance or choreography.

muscular endurance—Length of time that you can call on a particular muscle or muscle group to perform.

muscular strength—Capacity of muscles to perform.

natural form—A form of the choreography that follows a pattern found in nature, such as the progression of the seasons.

Nikolais, Alwin (1910-1993)—Founder of Nikolais Dance Theater. Known for his extensive and innovative use of props and set as integral elements in the choreography.

nonlocomotor—Movements that are stationary (do not travel through space).

parallel—Using the legs with the toes facing forward and the knees lined up over the toes.

parallel first—Position of the feet where the toes face forward of the body, the weight is evenly distributed on both feet, and the feet are positioned under the hips.

parallel fourth—Position of the feet where the toes face forward of the body with one foot forward of the other so that the heel of the forward foot is slightly forward of the toes of the back foot. Can be repeated on both sides.

parallel second—Position of the feet where the toes face forward of the body and the legs are separated slightly wider than the hips.

personal space—Area immediately around your body as you stand in place and travel through space.

Pilobolus Dance Theatre—Dance company that makes its highly athletic and visually striking dances through group collaboration.

plié—French term for bending the knees.

pointed foot—Toes extended forward, forming a straight line from the shin.

polycentrism—Movement that originates in several places or centers in the body, such as hips, ribs, and neck, simultaneously.

polyrhythmic music—Contains multiple rhythms in a single piece of music.

posterior—Back of the body or back of a part of the body.

power—Ability to produce maximum force in a short period of time.

prance—Briskly paced stylized walk where the feet are presented in front of the body rather than directly under the legs.

PRICED—Acronym for a method of healing an injury. The letters stand for protect, rest, ice, compression, elevation, and diagnosis.

process-oriented approach—Way of learning or creating in which the teacher provides ideas to explore that guide the student through his or her own learning. This way of teaching focuses on the learning itself rather than a specific product, like a performance.

prone—Lying facedown.

proprioception—Ability of the body to sense the position, location, orientation, and movement of its parts.

quick—Movements of a short duration within the time effort. The opposite of sustained.

reaction time—How quickly the body responds to an impulse or stimulus.

rebound—Responding to the natural momentum of the movement. This frequently means bouncing back to the opposite direction of the movement.

reflection—Act of thinking about your own actions, progress, habits, and behaviors. This can be an effective tool for technical improvement and assessment of your progress.

release—Returning to a neutral position after a contraction or arch.

relevé (demi-pointe)—Standing on the balls of your feet with your heels lifted off of the floor.

repetition—To repeat all or parts of a movement phrase or motif.

rondo—A musical and dance form in a verse-and-chorus structure, taking on the form ABACADA, where A represents the chorus. Can be repeated with any number of verses.

rotation—Turning the anterior surface of the muscle either inward or outward.

sagittal plane—Also known as the wheel plane. (Think of the way a wheel rolls down the street.) Composed of forward-and-back (sagittal dimension) and some side-to-side movements.

second position of the arms—Both arms held at a 90-degree angle to the torso, with a slight curve to the elbows, palm either forward or slightly tilted downward.

second position on the floor—Sitting upright on the floor with your legs open as wide as possible without inward rotation of the legs.

second position, or turned-out second—Position of the feet and legs in which the feet are set slightly wider than the hips with rotated, or turned-out, legs.

Shawn, Ted (1891-1972)—Early modern dance pioneer known for promoting men in modern dance and cofounding Denishawn, the first school of modern dance.

skill-related fitness—Coordination, agility, balance, power, reaction time, and speed.

skip—Traveling through space by alternating a step and a hop. One of the seven basic locomotor movements.

slide—Traveling through space sideways by alternating opening and closing the legs and feet. One of the seven basic locomotor movements.

somatic—Literally "of the body," but more commonly physical practices that recognize the integration of mind, body, and spirit.

space—Laban term for the way a person relates to space. Could be direct or indirect.

spatial sense—Ability to understand how your body is oriented in space and how the parts of your body are positioned with respect to the space and one another.

speed—Ability to propel the body from one place to another.

splicing—Inserting different or new material into the existing movement motifs.

stabile—Being completely on balance.

stage directions—Directions that actors, dancers, choreographers, directors, and designers use to identify locations on the stage. These are upstage, downstage, stage left, and stage right.

St. Denis, Ruth (1879-1968)—One of the matriarchs of modern dance. Known for introducing Eastern dance vocabulary into the modern dance lexicon. Also helped to popularize modern dance through wide exposure in vaudeville.

strong—Movement in which there is a lot of firmness and power or indulgence in gravity in the weight effort. The opposite of light.

study—Dance that is created as a preliminary experiment for learning choreographic skills or as preparation for a larger work.

successive—Movement that articulates or bends each joint along the way. In the case of the arm this means moving the shoulder, elbow, then wrist in order or the reverse. In the case of the leg, this means moving the hip, knee, and then ankle or the reverse.

supine—Lying faceup.

suspension—Ability to control the peak moment of balance.

sustained—Movements of a long duration within the time effort. The opposite of quick.

tailor sit—Seated position with the soles of the feet facing and touching one another.

Taylor, Paul (1930-)—Founder of the Paul Taylor Dance Company. Widely known for his large range of choreographic styles, topics, and music choices.

tempo—Speed at which movement or music is performed.

tendon—Tissue that attaches muscles to the bones.

Tharp, Twyla (1941-)—Founder of the Twyla Tharp Dance Foundation. A prolific and commercially successful choreographer known for her fusion of dance vocabularies and intricate timing in choreography.

theme and variation—A dance form where the choreographer develops a thematic phrase or movement material and alters it throughout the composition.

third position of the arms—One arm is held at a 90-degree angle to the side of the torso, the second arm is held in front of the chest with the middle finger lined up with the sternum. Both arms have a slight curve at the elbow and wrist.

third position, or turned-out third—Position of the feet and legs where the legs are rotated outward and one foot is placed so that the heel of that foot bisects the midline of the opposite foot.

three-step turn—Turn that alternates feet while turning. The first step takes you to face the back, the second step returns you to front, the third step finishes the turn by bending your knee so that you can repeat the turn to the alternate side.

tilt—Standing position where the shoulders remain over the hips, the arms are extended out from the body at shoulder height, and the entire body shifts to one leg without bending the torso.

time—Laban term for our perception of how fast or slowly we are moving. Time is either quick or sustained.

triplet—Series of three steps, usually with the pattern of down–up–up. In the down step the knees are bent, and in an up step the knees are straight and the heel is raised.

turned-out position—Rotation of the legs up to 180 degrees. The feet and legs are rotated away from the center line of the body as far as the hips will permit.

turnout—Rotation of the legs and feet outward from the midline of the body.

twist—Movement of the torso in which the shoulders move in the opposite direction from the hips.

unison—Everyone moving together doing the same thing at the same time.

unity—The cohesiveness or consistency in a dance.

variety—Using many types of movements and shapes in a dance.

vertical plane—Also known as the door plane. (Think of standing in a doorway and reaching your arms and legs to each of the corners.) This plane is composed of up-and-down (vertical dimension) and some side-to-side movements.

visual memory—Ability to remember what you see. In dance this often refers to remembering sequences of movement that you have viewed.

weight—The Laban term for the effect of gravity on the body. Weight can be strong or light.

Wigman, Mary (1886-1973)—German modern dance pioneer. A pupil of Laban, she was known as a powerful performer as well as the founder of the Wigman School of Dance in Germany.

X—Based on the work of Irmgard Bartenieff. A position where the dancer is lying on the back with feet and arms extended to the four diagonals of a square room.

References and Resources

Alter, M.J. (1998). *Sport stretch: 311 stretches for 41 sports.* Champaign, IL: Human Kinetics.

Anderson, J. (1992). *Ballet & modern dance: A concise history.* Princeton, NJ: Princeton Books.

Anderson Sofras, P. (2006). *Dance composition basics: Capturing the choreographer's craft.* Champaign, IL: Human Kinetics.

Aschenbrenner, J. (2002). *Katherine Dunham: A dancing life.* Champaign, IL: University of Illinois Press.

Autard, J.S. (2004). *Dance composition.* New York: Routledge.

Bailey, C. (1994). *Smart exercise.* New York: Houghton Mifflin.

Bales, M., & Nettl-Fiol, R. (Eds.) (2008). *The body eclectic: Evolving practices in dance training.* Chicago: University of Chicago Press.

Blom, L.A., & Chapin, L.T. (1982). *The intimate act of choreography.* Pittsburgh: University of Pittsburgh Press.

Bremser, M., Ed. (1999). *Fifty contemporary choreographers.* New York: Routledge.

Brown, J.M., Mindlin, N., Woodford, C.H., Eds. (1998). *The vision of modern dance.* Princeton, NJ: Princeton Books.

Buckroyd, J. (2000). *The student dancer: Emotional aspects of the teaching and learning of dance.* London: Dance Books.

Chemlar, R.D., & Fitt, S.S. (1990). *Diet for dancers: A complete guide to nutrition and weight control.* Highstown, NJ: Princeton Books.

Cheney, G. (1989). *Basic concepts in modern dance: A creative approach.* Princeton, NJ: Princeton Books.

Clippinger, K. (2007). *Dance anatomy and kinesiology.* Champaign, IL: Human Kinetics.

Coe, R. (1985). *Dance in America.* New York: Dutton.

Cohen, S.J. (1965). *The modern dance: Seven statements of belief.* Middletown, CT: Wesleyan University Press.

Cohen, S.J. (1972). *Doris Humphrey: An artist.* Princeton, NJ: Princeton Books.

Copeland, R. (2004). *Merce Cunningham: The modernizing of modern dance.* New York: Routledge.

Cunningham, M. (1984). *The dancer and the dance.* New York: Boyars.

Cunningham, M. (1997). The function of a technique for dance. In D. Vaughn (Ed.), *Merce Cunningham: Fifty years* (p. 60). New York: Aperture.

Duncan, I. (1928). *My life.* London: Gollancz.

Dunford, M. (Ed.) (2006). *Sports nutrition: A practice manual for professionals.* 5th ed. Chicago: American Dietetic Association.

Feuerstein, G. (2008). *The yoga tradition: Its history, literature, philosophy and practice.* Prescott, AZ: Hohm Press.

Fonteyn, M. (1979). *The magic of dance.* New York: Knopf.

Foulkes, J. (2002). *Modern bodies: Dance and American modernism from Martha Graham to Alvin Ailey.* Chapel Hill, NC: University of North Carolina Press.

Franklin, E. (2014). *Dance imagery for technique and performance.* 2nd ed. Champaign, IL: Human Kinetics.

Graham, M. (1991). *Blood memory: An autobiography.* New York: Bantam, Doubleday, Dell.

Hackney, P. (2002). *Making connections: Total body integration through Bartenieff fundamentals.* New York: Routledge.

Hodes, S. (1998). *A map of making dances.* New York: Ardsley.

Horosko, M. (2002). *Martha Graham: The evolution of her dance theory and training.* Gainesville, FL: University of Florida Press.

Humphrey, D. (1959). *The art of making dances.* Princeton, NJ: Princeton Books.

Humphrey, D. (2008). *New dance: Writings on modern dance.* Hightstown, NJ: Princeton Book Company.

Humphrey, D., & Cohen, S.J. (Eds). (1995). *Doris Humphrey: An artist first.* Princeton, NJ: Princeton Books.

Jones, B.T., & Kuklin, S. (1998). *Dance.* New York: Hyperion Books for Children.

Kassing, G. (2007). *History of dance: An interactive approach.* Champaign, IL: Human Kinetics.

Kassing, G., & Jay, D.M. (2003). *Dance teaching methods and curriculum design: Comprehensive K-12 dance education.* Champaign, IL: Human Kinetics.

Kirstein, L., Stuart, M., & Balanchine, G. (2004). *The classic ballet: Basic technique and terminology.* New York: Knopf.

Langer, E. (1989). *Mindfulness.* Cambridge, MA: Da Capo Books.

Langer, E. (1997). *The power of mindful learning.* Cambridge, MA: Da Capo Books.

Lavender, L. (1996). *Dancers talking dance: Critical evaluation in the choreography class.* Champaign, IL: Human Kinetics.

Legg, J. (2011). *Introduction to modern dance techniques.* Princeton, NJ: Princeton Books.

Legg, J. (May/June 2008). Katherine Dunham technique. *Dance Spirit* (12) 5:74.

Lerman, Liz. (2003). *Critical response process.* Takoma Park, MD: Liz Lerman Dance Exchange.

Lewis, D. (1984). *The illustrated dance technique of José Limón.* New York: Harper & Row.

Lillie, D. (November 2010). Katherine Dunham: Dancer, choreographer, educator, activist and innovator. *Dance Teacher* (32) 11:14.

Limón, J. (1998). *An unfinished memoir.* Middletown, CT: Wesleyan University Press.

Love, P. (1997). *Modern dance terminology.* Princeton, NJ: Princeton Books.

Martin, J. (1953, Apr. 12). The dancer as an artist. *New York Times* (1923-Current File), pp. SM19. http://search.proquest.com/docview/112854038?accountid=10559.

Mazo, J. (1977). *The prime movers.* Princeton, NJ: Princeton Books.

Minton, S.C. (2007). *Choreography: A basic approach using improvisation.* Champaign, IL: Human Kinetics.

Murray, J. (1979). *Dance now: A closer look at the art of movement.* New York: Penguin Books.

Nagrin, D. (1997). *The six questions: Acting technique for dance performance.* Pittsburgh: University of Pittsburgh Press.

Nagrin, D. (2001). *Choreography and the specific image.* Pittsburgh: University of Pittsburgh Press.

Newlove, J., & Dalby, J. (2004). *Laban for all.* New York: Routledge.

Perpener, J.O. (2001). *African-American concert dance: The Harlem Renaissance and beyond.* Champaign, IL: University of Illinois Press.

Pierre, D.B. (2005). A talk with Katherine Dunham. In V.A. Clark and S.E. Johnson (Eds.), *Kaiso! Writings by and about Katherine Dunham* (p. 249). Madison: University of Wisconsin Press.

Ross, J. (2000). *Moving lessons: Margaret H'Doubler and the beginning of dance in American education.* Madison: University of Wisconsin Press.

Siegel, M. (1969). Agents of change. Monograph. *Dance Perspectives* 38.

Solomon. R., Solomon, J., & Minton, S.C. (Eds.) (2005). *Preventing dance injuries.* Champaign, IL: Human Kinetics.

Sorell, W. (1966). *The dance has many faces.* New York: Columbia University Press.

Warren, L. (1977). *Lester Horton: Modern dance pioneer.* New York: Marcel Dekker.

Watkins, A., & Clarkson, P. (1990). *Dancing stronger, dancing longer: A dancer's guide to improving technique and preventing injury.* Hightstown, NJ: Princeton Books.

Index

Note: The letters *f* and *t* after page numbers indicate figures and tables, respectively.